Zodiac Signs

The Ultimate Guide on Zodiac Sign

Compatibility

(Amazing Facts about Each Sign and Everything

You Need to Know About Lunar Houses, Birth

Charts)

Robert Johnson

Published By **Jackson Denver**

Robert Johnson

Zodiac Signs: The Ultimate Guide on Zodiac Sign Compatibility (Amazing Facts about Each Sign and Everything You Need to Know About Lunar Houses, Birth Charts)

ISBN 978-1-998769-77-3

Legal & Disclaimer

TABLE OF CONTENTS

Chapter 1: The History Of Zodiac 1

Chapter 2: Understanding Your Sign 26

Chapter 3: Complete Profile Of The 12 Zodiac Signs 36

Chapter 4: Love Compatibility Of The 12 Zodiac Signs 59

Chapter 5: Astrology And Elements 76

Chapter 6: The Air Symptoms – Gemini, Libra & Aquarius 131

Chapter 7: Aries - "Fight And To Be The Primary"... 152

Chapter 1: The History Of Zodiac

The zodiac part of astrology that turned into first documented at some stage in the Roman technology. The Roman zodiac changed into based totally on Babylonian and Hellenistic astronomy. The time period "zodiac" become derived from the Latin word zodiacus which means that "circle of animals". This is the cause why half of of the symptoms of the Roman zodiac were represented via animals even as the Chinese zodiac is represented entirely by animals. The records of zodiac signs and symptoms has a very lengthy history and this bankruptcy will discuss about the origins of the zodiac sign.

Babylonian Period

The division of the ecliptic – the circle that contains the sun's orbit – into zodiac signs and symptoms started in the course of the Babylonian civilization throughout the first millennium BC. The Babylonian astronomers advanced the primary celestial coordinate device. The astronomical diaries of Babylonia were given with reference to the 3600 ecliptic. The Babylonian zodiac become also reflected in the Hebrew bible within the books of Revelations and Ezekiel specifically the zodiac symptoms of the lion (Leo) and bull (Taurus). On the other hand, many expert authors agree with that the tale of the twelve tribes of Israel changed into primarily based at the Babylonian zodiac. Moreover, many authors consider that the organized of the tribes around the tabernacle corresponds to the order of the Babylonian zodiac sign.

Greek and Roman Period

The Babylonian zodiac heavily encouraged the Roman zodiac throughout the 4th century BC. The adoption of the Roman empire of the Babylonian and Egyptian astrology gave upward thrust to the improvement of the western horoscopic astrology. One of the maximum famous astrology at some point of this era became Ptolemy whose work entitled Tetrabiblos become created out of the western astrological tradition. In fact, beneath Ptolemy, the houses as well as signal of the zodiac had been rationalized and set down in the sort of way that little has changed on it till nowadays.

Hindu Zodiac

The zodiac isn't always most effective used inside the western hemisphere. In truth, even the ones in India practice the belief of Hindu zodiac. The Hindu zodiac was primarily based on sidereal coordinate system that makes use of constant stars as references. Since the Hindu zodiac makes use of constant stars, it does no longer hold seasonal alignment in comparison to Babylonian, Greek and Roman zodiac. Moreover, the signs and symptoms of the Hindu zodiac additionally have extraordinary sounds with the Greek and Roman signs but, interesting enough, the symbols used are nearly same. For instance, the phrase dhanu in Hindu zodiac manner bow that represents Sagittarius inside the western zodiac.

Chinese Zodiac

The Chinese civilization has practiced the belief of zodiac signs on the grounds that time immemorial. The Chinese zodiac has a similar concept with western zodiac however it is totally exclusive from it. This particular zodiac uses a scheme in addition to systematic plan that correspond to a 12-12 months mathematical cycle. Thus, every 12 months corresponds to at least one zodiac signal. Moreover, the zodiac sign is also represented entirely via animals in contrast to western zodiac that is represented with the aid of animals, people and mythical creatures. The Chinese zodiac is noticeably famous in nations like Korea, Vietnam and Japan.

Modern Day Zodiac

The modern day zodiac become a revival of the Hellenistic (Greek) and Roman zodiac. It came round throughout the middle a long time. In reality, the zodiac was observed in lots of medieval stained glass in Cathedrals and castles. Modern day zodiac still uses the signs and symbols that had been advanced for the duration of the Greek and Roman length.

The zodiac signal is hard to understand specially amongst first timers. However, you don't need to strain about the unique symptoms and beneath is a desk that indicates the summary of the twelve zodiac symptoms with reference to its Greek, Hindu and Babylonian name. Another table will also be provided for the Chinese zodiac.

Table 1. The twelve zodiac symptoms on the subject of Greek, Hindu and Babylonian astrology.

Symbol Long Latin name English translation Greek Hindu Babylonian
♈ 0° Aries Ram Krios Meṣha LUHUNGA "The Agrarian Worker",
♉ 30° Taurus Bull Tavros Vṛiṣhabha GUANNA "The Steer of Heaven"
♊ 60° Gemini Twins Didymo Mithuna MASTABBAGALGAL "The Great Twins"
♋ ninety° Cancer Crab Karkinos Karkaṭa ALLUL "The Crayfish"
♌ a hundred and twenty° Leo Lion Leōn Siṃha UGRULA "The Lion"
♍ one hundred fifty° Virgo Maiden Parthenos Kanyā ABSIN "The Furrow"
♎ a hundred and eighty° Libra Scales Zygos Tulā ZIBBABBA "The Scales"

5

♏ 210° Scorpio Scorpion Skorpios Vṛśhchika GIRTAB "The Scorpion"

♐ 240° Sagittarius Centaur Archer Toxotēs Dhanuṣha PABILSAG "The soldier"

♑ 270° Capricorn Goat (Sea goat) Aigokerōs Makara SUHURMAS "The Goat-Fish"

♒ three hundred° Aquarius Water-Bearer Hydrokhoos Kumbha GULLA "The Great One",

♓ 330° Pisces Fish[27] Ikhthyes Mīna DUNUNU "The fish-cord"

Table 2. The twelve Chinese zodiac symptoms and their corresponding western zodiac.

Season Lunar month Animal Fixed element Solar longitude Gregorian date
Equivalent.
Western zodiac
Spring 1st 寅 (yin) Tiger Wood 314° Feb 4 – Feb 18 Aquarius
329° Feb 19 – Mar 5 Pisces
2d 卯 (mao)Rabbit Wood 344° Mar 6 – Mar 20
0° Mar 21 – Apr 4 Aries
3rd 辰 (chen)Dragon Earth 14° Apr five – Apr 19
29° Apr 20 – May four Taurus

Summer 4th 巳 (si) Snake Fire 44° May 5 – May 20
59° May 21 – Jun 5 Gemini
fifth 午 (wu) Horse Fire 74° Jun 6 – Jun 20
89° Jun 21 – Jul 6 Cancer
6th

 –未 (wei) Goat Earth 104° Jul 7 – Jul 22
119° Jul 23 – Aug 6 Leo
Autumn 7th 申 (shen)Monkey Metal 134° Aug 7 – Aug 22
149° Aug 23 – Sep 7 Virgo
eighth 酉 (you)Rooster Metal 164° Sep 8 – Sep 22
181° Sep 23 – Oct 7 Libra
9th 戌 (xu) Dog Earth 194° Oct 8 – Oct 22
211° Oct 23 – Nov 6 Scorpio
Winter tenth 亥 (hai) Pig Water 224° Nov 7 – Nov 21
244° Nov 22 – Dec 6 Sagittarius
11th 子 (zi) Rat Water 251° Dec 7 – Dec 21
271° Dec 22 – Jan five Capricorn
12th 丑 (chou) Ox Earth 284° Jan 6 – Jan 19
301° Jan 20 – Feb three Aquarius

Understanding The Astrological Signs

In the western astrology, the zodiac symptoms are closely influenced by way of one of a kind astrological signs. Astrological symptoms talk to the twelve three hundred sectors of the ecliptic which starts offevolved on the vernal equinox. The vernal equinox starts offevolved at Aries which is its first point observed via Taurus, Gemini, Cancer, Leo, Virgo, Libra, Scorpio, Sagittarius, Capricorn, Aquarius and Pisces in entire order. It is vital to take word that the zodiac signs and symptoms are closely encouraged with exceptional factors such as the motion of the planets, solar and moon. Moreover, it is also crucial to take notice that zodiac values the significance of ascendant which refers back to the growing on the east at the moment of a selected man or woman's delivery. This is the motive why special humans have distinctive characteristics, temperaments and destinies even supposing they may be born from beneath the equal star. This bankruptcy will talk approximately the distinct astrological signs and symptoms worried in zodiac signs and symptoms.

A. Western Zodiac

The western zodiac has a sturdy focus on the ascendant of an individual with admire to the twelve houses. This approach that astrologers can make predictions based totally on the beginning charts of someone. This segment will discuss approximately the different elements that have an impact on western zodiac.

The Four Elements (Polarity)

There are 4 factors involved in western zodiac – hearth, earth, water and air. These factors had been recognized by means of Greek philosopher Empedocles all through the fifth century BC. These factors constitute the opposing ideas of affection and strife. Having stated this, the exclusive mixtures and proportions of those elements create extraordinary natures of factors. He additionally referred to that people who are born with identical proportions of the elements are greater shrewd because they're stable.

The four factors are grouped in step with their polarity such that fireside and air indicate masculine signs and symptoms (effective and extrovert) even as water and earth imply feminine signs and symptoms (poor and introvert). Below is a chart that explains in detail the 4 factors in western zodiac.

Table 3. The description of the specific factors that affect the western zodiac with their corresponding, symbols, traits and signs and symptoms.

Polarity Element Characteristics Signs
Positive
(self-expressive) Fire Shows enthusiasm. Is pushed to express self and religion. Aries
Leo
 Sagittarius
Air Have top conversation and socialization abilties. Can also conceptualize things. Gemini
Libra
Aquarius
Negative

(self-containing) Earth Is practical and careful. Is also without difficulty tempted in material things. Taurus
Virgo
Capricorn

Water Is emotional. This element also makes a person extra emphatic and sensitive to the needs of others. Cancer
Scorpio Pisces

The classification consistent with those factors is very vital and astrologers usually start their interpretation based on the natal chart of individuals with their corresponding relationships with the placement and angles of planets.

Three Modalities

All of the four elements additionally appear distinct modalities. The three modalities include Cardinal, Fixed and Mutable. Below is a list of the unique modalities that impact the zodiac signs:

• The cardinal modality describes people to be initiative and these encompass human beings beneath the signs and symptoms Aries, Cancer, Libra and Capricorn.
• The fixed modality describes folks that are resistant to change and has top notch strength of mind. The signs and symptoms

that fall below this modality encompass Taurus, Leo, Scorpio and Aquarius.

• The mutable modality refers to folks that are adaptive together with the ones belonging to the signs and symptoms of Gemini, Virgo, Sagittarius and Pisces.

It is essential to take be aware that the exclusive elements want to mix with the 3 modalities to provide basic characterization. To make it less complicated, beneath is a chart that shows the relationship of the specific elements and modalities.

Table four. The courting of the four elements and three modalities.

Modalities with corresponding elements Air Fire Water Earth
Cardinal Libra Aries Cancer Capricorn
Fixed Aquarius Leo Scorpio Taurus
Mutable Gemini Sagittarius Pisces Virgo

Planetary Rulership

Planetary rulership refers to the connection among the correlated signal and the planets.

Western astrology believes that every zodiac sign is ruled by one of the seven seen planet which consist of the Sun, Moon, Mars, Venus, Mercury, Jupiter and Saturn. The conventional rulership of signs and symptoms is listed in the table under:

Table 5. The planetary rulership of the distinctive zodiac signs in western astrology.

Symbol
  Sign names Ruling
celestial body
(Classic astrology)
Ruling
celestial frame
(Modern astrology)
♈ Aries Mars Mars
♉ Taurus Venus Venus
♊ Gemini Mercury Mercury
♋ Cancer Moon Moon
♌ Leo Sun Sun
♍ Virgo Mercury Mercury
♎ Libra Venus Venus
♏ Scorpio Mars Pluto
♐ Sagittarius Jupiter Jupiter
♑ Capricorn Saturn Saturn

♒ Aquarius Saturn Uranus
♓ Pisces Jupiter Neptune

On the opposite hand, astrologers trust that the opposite planets that have been not blanketed inside the list serve as co-rulers. For example, Uranus is co-ruler of Aquarius at the same time as Neptune is co-ruler of Pisces. Lastly, Pluto is a co-ruler of Scorpio. This is the motive why the planetary rulership is special for each conventional and modern astrology. There is a lot of dialogue on the subject of which planetary rulership need to be followed however many astrologists have now tailored consequently they now observe the modern-day planetary rulership.

Essential Dignity

The planetary rulership provides a whole lot of impact to the sign that they rile. In western astrology, the belief of essential dignity is termed to the strength of the affect of the celestial body to the zodiac sign. Below are the 4 categories of Essential Dignity that you need to know:

• Dignity: A planet is taken into consideration bolstered or dignified if it falls beneath the zodiac signal that it regulations. For example, Mars is stated to exercise its rulership if the zodiac that it policies encompass Aries and Scorpio.

• Detrimental: This refers to a planet this is under the sign contrary to what it should rule. This manner that the planet is weakened because it can't workout its rulership nicely and because the zodiac sign that falls below it is not compatible. For example, Mars on Taurus is considered as a unfavorable rulership.

• Exaltation: A planet can also be strengthened while it's miles in the signal of exaltation. Exaltation refers to a degree of dignity that is exaggerated as compared to rulership. Exaltation is supposed to give the planet dignity. Examples of planets of their Exaltation consist of Sun (Aries), Saturn (Libra), Venus (Pisces), Mercury (Virgo) and Moon (Taurus).

• Fall: This term is opposite to exaltation. Thus, it refers back to the planet being weakened.

To apprehend similarly, beneath is a table that summarizes the position of planets and suns in keeping with the notion of Essential Dignity.

Table 6. Table summarizing the placement of planets with corresponding strengths and weaknesses based totally at the notion of Essential Dignity.

Planet	Symbol	Detriment	Dignity	Fall	Exaltation
Sun		Aquarius	Leo	Libra	Aries
Moon		Capricorn	Cancer	Scorpio	Taurus
Mercury		Sagittarius and Pisces	Gemini and Virgo	Leo	Aquarius
Venus		Aries and Scorpio	Libra and Taurus	Virgo	Pisces
Mars		Libra and Taurus	Aries and Scorpio	Cancer	Capricorn
Jupiter		Gemini and Virgo	Sagittarius and Pisces	Capricorn	Cancer
Saturn		Cancer and Leo	Capricorn and Aquarius	Aries	Libra

B. Horoscopic House System

The horoscope and zodiac are two interrelated things. The horoscope is an astrological diagram that represents the positions of the astrological aspects at a certain time or occasion. The maximum realistic use of horoscope is the interpretation of astrologer based totally at the movements of celestial bodies. In fact, you'll basically see horoscope from newspaper and magazines that supply trendy prediction based totally on the zodiac placement of the sun or moon. Having stated this, it's miles vital to also provide a discussion approximately horoscope.

The horoscope represents the extraordinary fields of reports wherein the energies of the planets and zodiac symptoms come into play that are then manifested within the bodily surroundings in addition to existence reviews of a person.

In order to create a horoscope, it's far vital that the astrologer determines the exact time as well as vicinity of someone's birth. The astrologer will then convert the time to sidereal time to calculate the midheaven and ascendant. This is observed by way of the calculation of the ephemeris which refers to area of the celestial bodies for a selected time based on sidereal time. Below are the features of the western horoscope.

House System

The 12 houses are known as the 12 divisions of the ecliptic on the time as well as location of the horoscope in query. The homes are numbers in counter clockwise from the primary house. In wellknown, the homes one to six are located underneath the horizon whilst the houses seven to 12 are placed above. It is crucial to take observe that the residence structures are heavily dependent upon the rotational motion of the Earth inside its axis. Although it's far hard to calculate the horoscope based totally on the house machine, beneath is a guide of the way the houses are interpreted.

Table 7. The precis of the house interpretation in horoscope as suffering from the zodiac signal.

House Zodiac Sign Title Interpretation

1st Aries House of Self The physical appearance and traits are important and they depart true first influence. This house also provides a wellknown appearance of the ego. It additionally represents the start of things.

2nd Taurus House of Value This house holds cloth and intangible things of price. This residence is right in handling money, homes and investments. The house also represents self-worth, cultivation and increase.

third Gemini House of Communications This refers back to the early improvement and youth surroundings. The 0.33 house represents happiness, accurate conversation, intelligence and achievements. It also represents the bond among siblings and associates. It additionally influences travel and transportation.

4th Cancer House of Home and Family This residence represents lineage and ancestry or the early basis of the circle of relatives and environment. This house seems at motherhood as a super determine because it looks after the household.

fifth Leo House of Pleasure Recreation and doing amusement activities are especially vital on this house. This house represents enjoyment, love, romance and self-expression.

sixth Virgo House of Health This house refers to responsibilities and duties. The skills and trainings that an character has obtained also are important in this residence. Under this residence consist of jobs, employment and the rendering of carrier to others.

seventh Libra House of Partnerships The house of partnership refers to shut relationship constructed on the inspiration of believe. It refers to relationships like marriage and commercial enterprise partners. Under this residence, agreements and diplomatic relationships also are being ruled.

8th Scorpio House of Reincarnation This residence represents the cycle of demise and rebirth. Moreover, sexual relationships and deeply dedicated courting also are blanketed. This house additionally rules the joint homes of partners. On the alternative hand, it additionally represents self-transformation and regeneration.

ninth Sagittarius House of Philosophy The ninth residence guidelines foreign tour, culture, long distance journeys, faith, law, ethics and better training. It is likewise represented through higher shape of knowledge through enlargement.

tenth Capricorn House of Social Status The tenth house refers to goals and motivations in your career. It additionally affects social fame, authority and authorities. This house is represented by the father parent that's its best symbol.

11th Aquarius House of Friendships The 11th house is the House of Friendship for this reason it values associates of like-minded people. It also represents agencies, clubs and social businesses.

12th Pisces House of Self-Undoing This residence represents mystery. It additionally represents places where people are secluded or isolated along with within the health facility and prison. Moreover, it additionally represents the things that are visible to oneself but certainly visible with the aid of other people. This residence additionally represents the elusive and secretive behavior of humans.

Aspects

The aspect refers back to the relative angles between the pairs of planets that rule a specific signal. The greater specific issue discovered, the extra critical the connection is. There are forms of elements and those encompass the exact and real. The distinction among the two is known as an orb. The orb is differentiated based totally at the angles that it produces. For instance, a 1800 is referred to as a conjunction even as a 900 distinction is a rectangular.

Ascendant

The ascendant (ASC) refers back to the point of the ecliptic plane that rises from the east. This time period may be very important in the interpretation of horoscope as it exerts more energy as compared to the solar, moon and other celestial our bodies. It is, in fact, the primary point of power within the natal life accordingly it provides the expression of who we are as individuals.

C. Chinese Zodiac

Unlike western zodiac, the Chinese zodiac symptoms are not assigned to ecliptic sections and did now not originate from constellations. Instead, the Chinese zodiac operates on distinct time cycles – years, lunar months and two-hour duration of days. The Chinese zodiac has 5 elements that balance the exceptional symptoms. Below is a discussion of the vital five factors inside the Chinese zodiac.

• Wood: Wood is characterised by having high moral and self assurance. It is also attributed to having wide variety of interests as well as idealistic dreams. The route that s favorable to this detail is the east that's the season of spring. It is the element for the animal symptoms of Rabbit and Tiger.

• Earth: This element is characterized by way of having logical and methodical intelligence. A man or woman who has an excellent amount of earth in his or her persona is ideal at planning. The path associated with this detail is the center thinking about that this detail governs the 4 seasons. It is the detail that policies the Dragon, Ox, Goat and Dog.

• Fire: Fire is related to aggressiveness and passion consequently a person who has this element own brilliant management talents and is definitely assertive. The route of this detail is south that's in connection with the summer time. This is the detail that guidelines the animal sign of Horse and Snake.

• Water: The water detail is characterized via having a persuasive and emphatic function. A person who has this element is goal. The route associated with the detail is North that's the season for iciness. The animal signs and symptoms dominated with the aid of this detail are rat and pig.

• Metal: Metal is characterised via constant values, evaluations and sincerity. The route that is associated with this detail is north that is autumn. This element regulations the signs and symptoms of Rooster and Monkey.

The five elements operate collectively with the twelve animal signs and symptoms inside a 60-yr calendar. The elements exist inside the calendar with their yin and yang bureaucracy. The yin years confer with years that cease with even numbers and they may be represented via femininity and passiveness. The yang, alternatively, is made of years that lead to peculiar numbers and are represented by using masculinity and light. Below is a desk that summarizes the twelve

Chinese zodiacs and the elements that rule them.

Table 8. The twelve signs and symptoms of Chinese zodiac and their corresponding elements and forms

Sign Form Element Direction Season
Rat Yang Water North Mid-Winter
Ox Yin Water North Late Winter
Tiger Yang Wood East Early Spring
Rabbit Yin Wood East Mid-Spring
Dragon Yang Wood East Late Spring
Snake Yin Fire South Early Summer
Horse Yang Fire South Mid-Summer
Goat Yin Fire South Late Summer
Monkey Yang Metal West Early Autumn
Rooster Yin Metal West Mid-Autumn
Dog Yang Metal West Late Autumn
Pig Yin Water North Early Winter

Chapter 2: Understanding Your Sign

Just because you're interested in understanding approximately your signal, this does not mean that you need to study notably to apprehend astrology. There are realistic processes to understanding how the zodiac signs and symptoms work and this bankruptcy will speak approximately the principles and widespread traits that govern the twelve zodiac signs.

Aries

Aires is symbolized through the ram which represents the male fertility as well as courage and aggression. The ram's horn is taken into consideration as part of the cornucopia as a result it's miles dubbed because the horn of lots. People who are born below this signal have the affinity closer to abundance.

Sun in Aries human beings are born as herbal athletes. They are energetic, active, straightforward and not complex. They are people who recognise what they need and how they can achieve them. On the opposite hand, the moon can also play a critical role in affecting their behavior. For instance, Moon in Aries people are extremely impatient as a consequence they live for the instant and infrequently has the endurance to watch for matters to occur. This is the reason why they are proactive in solving their problems due to the fact they want to look the results right now. In trendy, individuals who are born under this signal are competitive, short and direct.

Taurus

Taurus has always been the image of power and strength. Taureans are believed to be sturdy individuals but although they may be reliable due to the fact they have got the dependancy of being outright beneficial. They are also clearly sensual humans in all pleasure regions and they take pleasure on just about something like food, a cushty blanket or even flora. Since they enjoy things that provide them consolation, additionally they have the tendency to enjoy material matters. Since they're strong-willed people, it's far unwise to push humans born underneath this famous person to do matters that they may be not committed. However, once they're committed to doing matters, they placed all their time, energy and effort to doing matters. This is the purpose why human beings born under this megastar are very captivated with love and romance.

Gemini

Geminis are seemed to have dual nature as this signal is symbolized by way of twins. However, the duality is frequently expressed within the alternate and interplay of Geminis with different human beings. Geminis are very flexible human beings and their ability to adapt to adjustments makes them very clean to address. This is the motive why individuals who are born beneath this famous person are very pleasant, witty and smart. However, under the lunar role, Geminis have worrisome behavior and that they need extra stimulation than different humans. This is the reason why they also can be overbearing on occasion. With their traits to continually ask questions, Geminis love to transport round freely and mingle with human beings to get answers to their questions.

Cancer

Being symbolized with the aid of the crab, folks that are born below this celebrity constantly circulate in indirect manner. They direct their lives toward wherein they could benefit quite a few blessings in their lives. This is the cause why they've robust survival instincts. They are also very protecting in particular in sharing their internal selves to many humans.

Cancers also have the popularity to be moody. This is clear to people who are born whilst the Moon is in Cancer. Although withdrawn, people who are born beneath this zodiac signal are thoughtful by way of nature. They are also sensitive to like and they can provide loads of factors to their loved ones like security, consolation and care. Overall, Cancers frequently move about with their enterprise without making a variety of noise. They are mild human beings that spend money on their inner selves more than some thing else.

Leo

The zodiac sign Leo is symbolized via the might lion which represents rulership, braveness and sovereignty. In fact, there may be an unmistakable regal air to individuals who are born below this famous person. They are dignified but additionally they have the reputation for being conceited. Although their outward look shows conceit, Leo are inspired with the aid of the affections of people surrounding her or him for this reason their plans usually middle round making folks who count number to them satisfied.

On the other hand, Leo humans also love being the middle of attention. Whether they are inner their homes or out with their pals, Leo people need to be always inside the spotlight. They also have the incessant need to be in control of factors and their all-controlling conduct can be difficult to bear with.

Virgo

Virgo humans are, in standard, first rate humans. The image, the virgin, is interpreted as having natural in spirit and additionally being self-contained. Virgos are reticent particularly once they face some thing new.

Virgos discover contentment, security and luxury in little things. They experience doing mundane responsibilities like paying payments or balancing their books. Having said this, many people under this signal are accused to be underachievers. The satisfaction that they get from simple things prevents them from pursuing amazing matters in existence. Although this may be the case, this is the first-class of Virgo human beings that makes them endearing.

Libra

People born beneath this signal are symbolized via the dimensions which represents balance. Librans are sociable and highbrow. Because they experience stability in their lives, they have a tendency to are seeking for the center ground hence they have got the tendency to become the whole thing for every person. They are also accused for having loss of directness and lack of ability to take a stable stand on matters.

Since Librans look for concord and peace, they have a tendency to concede on things and that they allow humans win in arguments. Their ability to try for balance makes them attractive and that is the reason why Libra natives additionally have tendencies to draw many human beings from the other intercourse effortlessly.

Scorpio

Scorpios are severe human beings and they are very determined on the subject of achieving the matters that they need to do. They are prompted by using electricity thus they have a number of willpower to do things. It is thrilling to take note, however, that Scorpios are very cunning humans. They don't exit and seize the things that they want at the wrong moment. Instead, they watch for the proper possibility. With this, Scorpios are excellent at making plans and scheming.

Sagittarius

Sagittarius are folks that are outgoing and friendly. The love freedom and that they abhor doing habitual works. Their love for making friends also places them at risk because they regularly have blind faith in people. Their optimism is infectious but this can also lead them to trouble now and again. Since Sagittarians are beneath the hearth sign, in addition they have brief tempers however, fortuitously, they quick forget the supply in their anger.

Sagittarians have the want for regular pastime and their outgoing persona makes them irresponsible. They without problems overlook appointments and they discover it hard to complete duties that they don't like. Although this may be the case, they can also come to be true teachers as they're correct in storytelling.

Capricorn

People born under this signal are grounded and practical. They also are more fixated on doing things that are worthwhile. They have near relationships with other Earth symptoms like Taurus and Virgo and that they want to be useful and powerful in society. Being beneficial in addition to productive is critical for Capricorns because they want to keep their emotions underneath take a look at. On the opposite hand, they can be at risk to having turbulent feelings and they are at hazard to being skeptic with other human beings.

Aquarius

Aquarius is below the solar signal and people below this zodiac revere the antique and traditional methods of doing matters. They have robust idealism for this reason they are likely to have constant reviews on everything. Unfortunately, that is the motive why maximum Aquarians are branded as standoffish people but this is only a façade. In truth, they are observant and tolerant in a wide sense. They are also very witty and intellectual human beings.

Pisces

Pisces incorporates all studies of all the zodiac signs. Thus, they've the capacity to communicate and identify with humans from all backgrounds. They are not handiest adaptable however additionally they have extensive minds. They also spend a number of their time craving for contentment. Because they yearn contentment, most Pisceans have the tendency to be dreamy and out of touch of reality. They additionally glamorize suffering.

Chapter 3: Complete Profile Of The 12 Zodiac

Signs

Everyone is particular. Each one people is endowed with specific behaviors and characteristics. These traits can be attributed to our zodiac sign. Notice that there are people inside your circle who can recognize you higher than everybody else. You might also come across people who by hook or by crook share the equal character as you with reference to what they prefer and what they trust in. This is due to the fact these people are most probable born below the equal signal as you or they'll be under a one-of-a-kind zodiac signal however they are well matched with your zodiac. On the opposite hand, there are the ones folks that simply can't appear to thrill you regardless of what they do. The motive is their personality profile may not be like minded with yours.

Here are the different persona profiles of each 12 zodiac symptoms:

Aries (Mar. 21- Apr. 20): As a fireplace sign, human beings born beneath the Aries signal are lively, adventurous and extraordinarily outgoing. They love adventure and they are complete of energy. Aries people own self assurance, enthusiasm, and braveness. They are very imaginitive, quick-witted and sharp. When it involves matters that they prefer, they are very passionate. They are clearly heat and fiery.

Although they're outgoing, forward and impartial, Aries people tend to be too naïve and trusting. There are times after they discover themselves putting their personal lives at hazard. Good aspect, they continually find a way to bounce back after every adversity. People born underneath this signal are quick-tempered. They own a robust sense of urgency and in order that they tend to be bossy, impulsive and impatient. They also are procrastinators and every now and then they can be self-focused.

Aries is the most masculine and bodily amongst all of the zodiac signs and symptoms. Women born underneath this sign are competitive, dynamic and forceful and this is essentially the purpose why maximum Aries girls discover themselves in complex situations with their companions. A guy has to be a "actual guy" to meet an Aries lady otherwise, he shall be intimidated through her. Likewise, a female has to be a "real girl" to fulfill an Aries man. Aries men look for a lady who can supplement his traits. They need a lady who can similarly percentage their passion but she must in no way answer returned.

Women born underneath Aries signal are the maximum intimidating of all of the zodiac symptoms. They are very thrilling, adventurous, aggressive and unbiased. Generally speaking, Aries human beings are impulsive thinkers and that's why they constantly encounter many dangers and accidents. When they talk, they are speakme from revel in and now not only a connection with something they read or heard. They hate to be limited and possessed. They love demanding situations and so while things are going well for them, they locate it uninteresting and so they will go out of their way to make their lifestyles exciting.

Taurus (Apr. 21- May 20): People born under the Taurus zodiac are the maximum charming and appealing among all zodiacs. They are generally beautiful human beings and that they constantly surround themselves with stunning matters. It could be very rare that a

Taurean will exit with out being nicely dressed. They are quite independent and intelligent. Among the first-rate traits of the Taurus humans are: Patience, reliability, extraordinarily loving nature, kindness, strong determination, love of material things and safety, creativity, independence, charisma, loyalty and top decision-making capabilities.

Tauruses can be famous amongst their peers and colleagues but they nonetheless control to discreetly shop a variety of time for themselves. Despite their reputation for being communal, they're nevertheless capable of stay far from the gang. People can best get as close to them as they intend them to be. When they're not within the mood to socialise, they can effortlessly close each person out from their life and revel in their personal solitude. Taurus humans are very stubborn and proud. When they already set their mind to something, nobody could be capable of budge them out of it. It will take numerous top and reasonable motives to convince a Taurus in any other case.

Taurus human beings are open-minded but they're no longer too trusting. They don't want their non-public life without problems violated. They are often judged as snobby and withdrawn because they tend to maintain things to themselves. They always preserve a fab and amassed outdoors. Only when Taurus lets you in on their lifestyles would you be capable of find out how a laugh it's far to be with them. Their feelings, goals, desires and fears run deeper than each person could dare discover.

Taurus people prioritize material comforts. They love lovely matters and that they ensure that they are surrounded with lovely and snug things. It is very regular for a Taurean to stay in a lovely house. It may not be a massive house however for a Taurean, it have to be comfortable, homey and delightful. They hate adjustments. Although they may be adaptable, they are no longer very fond of adjustments. They are not truely flexible. They have a tendency to be really possessive, jealous, resentful and egocentric. Taureans are sensual beings. Anything that is enjoyable to their senses (sight, contact, taste and odor) absolutely appeals to them. They love nature and are puppy-pleasant. They are very reliable. When they make a promise or when they say some thing, consider that a Taurean will without a doubt try this.

Gemini (May 21- Jun. 21): Gemini human beings are extremely adaptable and sociable. They are the most talkative humans most of the zodiacs. They can not stay in one area all of the time. They thirst for brand spanking new studies and getting to know and so that they have an internal desire to examine a piece of everything. Variety is what they crave for. They are well mannered, clever and active. People from the alternative zodiac signs love to speak about them at the side of Virgos and Scorpios. As a result, they're often dissected and dragged down by means of others. They are gifted however their without difficulty-apprehensive nature on occasion reasons people to decide them and placed them down.

Geminis are top notch in making-cash. They are mysterious and multi-proficient. This is exactly the purpose why Geminis regularly make human beings jealous of them. Their friends adore them and they may be super communicators. They are magnetic and bendy. They can resist some thing obstacle comes their way.

The poor developments of Geminis are being sick-tempered, impatient, moody, argumentative, inquisitive, superficial, cunning, and inconsistent. They are fickle-minded. Geminis are multi-taskers. They have the ability to supply something out of not anything but best accomplish that while they may be involved. As articulate as they're Geminis can easily convince people. They are the lifestyles of the party. They are very shrewd. In truth, if there's someone you need to ask for an answer to a tough pass-phrase puzzle, it have to be a Gemini. Lastly, Geminis want people in their circle to treat them with appreciate. They aren't resentful and they don't hold grudges for too lengthy.

Cancer (Jun. 22- July 22): Like their animal image – the crab- Cancers possess impenetrable outside but deep down inner they are one of the most touchy and emotional humans. They are full of contradictions. They are compassionate and caring when it comes to people who depend to them like their own family, buddies and fanatics however when they are jealous or moody they may be extremely rash, devious and quarrelsome. They may be unmindful of other's evaluations however they get simply touchy and emotional approximately how people can see them.

People born under this sign are very moody and that they will be inclined to be insecure and mawkish. They are probably the most mysterious people of the zodiac. Cancers are protecting in their cherished ones. They are notably innovative, innovative and intuitive. They have a tendency to be shielding of their cherished ones. They like to nurture humans and they're very useful too so long as they recognize they are not being taken advantage of.

Cancers are full of electricity. They are sensible and inventive. They fee their own freedom and they're brave humans.

When it comes to relationships, Cancers have a tendency to prioritize their family and loved ones over repute and fortune. They love journey. They are regularly pet-pleasant however can be truely enterprising at times.

Unlike the opposite brave signs of the zodiac, Cancers are not keen on taking dangers. Their safety is important to them and if they're now not positive approximately what they're coming into, Cancers will not possibly gamble. They are fond of cash and regularly, money is a finding out element of their relationships. They are romantic and no different symptoms can romance better than a most cancers. This enigmatic signal is clearly amusing to be with whilst you get to know them higher.

Leo (July 23- Aug. 22): People born underneath this sign are normally charismatic, beneficiant, faithful, enthusiastic, loving, broadminded, innovative and expansive. They are fortunate to have a charismatic persona as they appeal to opportunities and abundance in existence. If they are faced with any adversity, Leos can overcome their issues with their humorousness and style. They are very emotional in that they permit their coronary heart take manipulate in their moves and selections.

They are trustworthy and dependable. Once they start to devote in a courting, anticipate that a Leo will keep on with his partner via thick and thin. Caution and severe warning is needed to make the connection ultimate with Leos for once their trust is broken, it'll by no means be possible to repair it. No one would really like to mess around with a Lion. They aren't very forgiving. Once you harm a Leo, he'll in no way forgive and overlook. When Leos end their relationship, it's miles truely the quit. No more room for 2nd chances. They will depart you behind with out turning back. They can easily reduce their relationships and harm their associate however Leos will by no means try this without a very good reason. Once they bid you good-bye, it's miles sincerely goodbye for suitable.

Pride is Leo's weak point. When you strike their ego, you are genuinely in for a pleasant deal with however whilst you throw them criticisms, expect that Leos will in no way address you once more. They have a flamboyant personality. They are rigid and pompous. They have a huge tendency to expose off. They are hardworking and really generous. They can be the primary one to present you their coat when you're cold and be the primary to cheer you up whilst you're down.

People born beneath this sign are proud. They are born leaders and that they hate it a lot when any other man or woman attempts to dethrone them. They also are rather innovative. They like to constantly be the center of every body's attention. They are absolutely caring and emotional on the subject of the humans they love.

Virgo (Aug. 23- Sept. 23): People born under the Virgo sign are the maximum perfectionist and meticulous most of the complete zodiac. They are normally shy and modest. They are analytical, shrewd, reliable, diligent and sensible. Many astrologers do not regard Virgos enormously due to the fact they've the tendency to be slender-minded and fussy. But after they begin to excel, Virgos are the most creative, a hit and dependent among all Zodiac symptoms.

Virgos refuse to be cynical even if others flip their backs on them. They nevertheless accept as true with in the goodness of the people and this kindness is frequently taken advantage of by way of other more potent symptoms. Virgos are most usually mistreated and victimized by using their companions or friends. Virgos are commonly shy and in order that they in no way need to take the center stage. Instead, they allow others and their cherished ones experience the highlight and they'll be satisfied and contented looking them from the sidelines.

Virgos also are sensitive and sensitive. They also are innovative in their own right but may not be as creative as the other more dominant zodiac. As a pal, human beings born underneath this sign are faithful and they will no longer live you while you needed them the most. Since they recognize the way it feels to be left alone or mistreated, Virgos will stand via your side. They are reflective and deep. They are very expertise and worrying of these they preserve important in their life.

Virgos are enthusiastic about the idea of being in order. They are meticulous and perfectionist that's on occasion way over board. They can be fault-finders and naggers now and again and so they have a tendency to push others away. On the fantastic word, Virgos are punctual and reliable. They are extraordinarily sensible and as a depend of truth, many scientists and mathematicians are beneath this sign. As perfectionists, Virgos are especially highbrow. They generally tend to suppose deeply and they don't forestall till all topics are solved correctly. They are reserved and cool. They are very diplomatic and so they regularly earn the respect and believe in their buddies and co-workers.

Libra (Sept. 24- Oct. 22): Librans are the most romantic of all symptoms within the zodiac. Libra is ruled by way of Venus and so that they commonly own a hopeless romantic mentality. These are the those who put on their hearts on their sleeves. They trust in fairytale endings. They all dream about finding their prince or princess. People beneath this zodiac signal are typically nature-lovers, they love to journey and they're very sports activities-minded. They are fond of the movies, amusement and the humanities. Librans re very committed but they tend to be frivolous sometimes.

When it comes to their feelings, Librans regularly lose their exact judgment. They are impulsive and they locate trouble locating motive while they may be stuck in the game of love. Librans additionally will be inclined to be self-willed, envious, and egocentric. They are just and they aid the justice gadget and brotherhood but they typically fail to act in that branch.

Librans are regularly dubbed as two-faced due to the fact they're effortlessly distracted and swayed by means of exceptional views. They are just thinkers but they do not normally see it to fruition. When they experience that something is not going their manner, Librans will now not waste their time pursuing it. They are very indecisive and that makes them unreliable.

Those who're born under this sign are diplomatic, charming, sociable, adaptable, loving, generous, idealistic, clean-going, intuitive, proficient, perceptive and poised. On the negative note, Librans are easily prompted, flirtatious, quick-tempered, egocentric, self-indulgent, and they're very susceptible to daydream. They are very gullible and they hate monotony.

Scorpio (Oct. 23- Nov. 21): This solar sign is the most effective signal a number of the zodiac. Children born under this sign are known for his or her understanding beyond their age. Astrologers even call this sign as the "oldest soul". Scorpios locate it tough from time to time to discover the direction to their own happiness even though they have a tendency to have all of the answers. There are 3 fundamental necessities in the lifestyles of a Scorpio: power, preference and passion. All too frequently, Scorpios need to straighten out their confusion among love of power and strength of affection. People around them find it hard to address the Scorpio's sensitivity and emotional depths. It is possible to have a Scorpio for a partner for years and not definitely know them. They are difficult to read. They continually tend to hold most of the matters approximately them a mystery. Dealing with them isn't always easy for you have to do it in a deeper way nearly in an intuitive degree. Scorpios are very mysterious. It seems like they are always carrying a masks. Usually, when they are saying sure, it honestly way no. Their persona is contradicting. When a person crosses a Scorpio, they're absolutely in for an unpleasant surprise. Scorpio is one of the maximum envious signs. They by no means forgive and overlook.

People born below this sign are destined to be champions. The handiest flaw that often hinders them from attaining their desires is their attitude. The manner they assume could make or destroy them. When they set on some thing and Scorpio start to emerge as vital, it may truly get on their way leading to them no longer realizing their goals.

Scorpios make the fine leaders in the international. They go away no room for failure. They are forceful, dynamic and decided. They are emotional. When they do some thing they constantly set their coronary heart to it. When they love, they love difficult and after they live, they live difficult.

Scorpios possess a eager eye for detail and a strong thoughts with sturdy self-discipline. Their personality is enigmatic; that's why they are very famous with their peers. They are very passionate about the matters they love. They like nature.

Sagittarius (Nov. 22- Dec. 20): People born underneath the hunter's sign or the archer are the most optimistic some of the complete zodiac signs. When they locate some thing beautiful, they may set their minds to it and inside the technique, own it. They strongly agree with that the whole thing is feasible.

Sagittarians are dominated by way of the planet Jupiter and so they are constantly at the move. They are the happiest once they pursue some thing that entices them like a baby chasing a butterfly. It is truely hard to make this humans stay in one place and relax. They normally like to travel and maximum of them are interested in philosophical, outdoor and media pursuits. Sagittarians are protective when their experience of identity is violated. In relationships, their privateness wishes to be reputable. When they in the end locate their associate who is familiar with this predicament, Sagittarians may be the pleasant partner of all: beneficiant, amusing-loving and magnanimous.

Aside from optimism, human beings born underneath this signal are honest and freedom-loving. Many conflict heroes are

Sagittarians and that proves how patriotic they're. They have a captivating sense of humor and that makes them virtually fun to be with. They are superb and so they are glad maximum of the time. They have a robust experience of honor. They will by no means do anything cheating and likewise they may not tolerate it round their circle. They are dependable and law-abiding. When a person attempts to get into a Sagittarian's negative aspect, they could really be combative. People consider them due to the fact they may be sincere. They are honest and so they have a sturdy tendency to be frank and direct. They easily get indignant or irritated but this doesn't final long. They additionally don't hold grudges against humans.

Sagittarians are moody. They are tactless particularly when they feel the want to be direct. They are careless ad in order that they have a tendency to hurt human beings at instances with their phrases. Sagittarians have a propensity to take humans for granted. When their energy is not properly directed, they will sense disappointed and this ends in self-pity and vanity.

Capricorn (Dec. 21- Jan. 19): Capricornians are sensible, cool, bold, disciplined and really prudent. Anyone born underneath this sign will do everything of their strength to achieve their desires and gradually triumph over them. Their robust self-discipline and ambitious nature pushes them forward and up the ladder of success. When humans around them appear to be having their tough times, a Capricorn nonetheless manipulate to preserve a cool and calm character. He can concentrate to a long and disturbing rant but nonetheless be cool about it.

Capricorns desire to succeed in both love and existence. Although they may be conservative and cautious by nature, they nevertheless thread to unsure lands in their look for love and fulfillment. In relationships, Capricorns lengthy for lasting relationships. They are normally very difficult-working and they may be the most workaholic and purpose-oriented a number of the whole zodiac. They are inspired via energy, reputation, success, money and love.

As they always tend to be cautious, Capricorns do not easily get swayed to devote in a new dating. They need to test the waters first before they dive in it. Once they locate that they're secure, only then can the Capricorns screen their actual, sensitive and emotional nature. In friendships, Capricorns are one of the most reliable and sympathetic.

Their sense of humor is often sarcastic but it's far what makes them amusing to be with. In case of emergencies, Capricorns are in all likelihood to stay calm whilst all of the other loses their minds not knowing what to do. They are appealing in that they usually see to it that they're nicely-mannered fueled by means of their disciplined nature.

Capricorns have a tendency to preserve grudges on human beings. They are angered by using small things in preference to big ones. They have a tendency to be terrible thinkers, calculating, proud, egocentric, fatalistic and rigid. When they may be in a dating, Capricorns are very jealous and possessive.

Aquarius (Jan. 20- Feb. 18): The maximum magnanimous a number of the zodiac is the Aquarius. They are usually humanitarian and therefore it isn't sudden that most philanthropists are born underneath this signal. Aquarians are relatively independent. They are very pleasant, innovative, idealistic, rational, authentic, unswerving and resourceful. However, Aquarians also are rebellious in nature. They may be actually tactless, and whimsical. They are one of the maximum unpredictable signs and symptoms in the zodiac and because of this humans around them discover it difficult to assume in which they stand of their existence. This unpredictability makes an Aquarian clearly stressful at times but it's also why they may be captivating.

Aquarians are thinkers. They always pursue some thing on an highbrow stage. They are very mental and so they make the quality and maximum well-known inventors. Aquarians are trendsetters. Their tendency to technique matters on a mental degree can result to intense success and disaster. Many human beings protected on the Hall of Fame are undeniably Aquarians, but maximum human beings within the mental establishments also belong under this signal.

Aquarians are very humanitarian, outgoing, truthful judgment and amiable. They are one of the maximum mysterious humans within the zodiac and no Aquarians are precisely alike. Their thoughts may be very short and that they have a truly suitable memory. They are moody at instances. They usually leave a great impression on human beings they meet due to the fact they're high-quality. They are extremely adventurous and their minds are regularly complete of loopy stuff.

Aquarians, also have a propensity to position on a chilly shoulder due to their unpredictable nature. They every so often game a detach ecosystem around them making it certainly difficult for human beings to apprehend them. They love isolation maximum of the time and that they don't care approximately what other humans think of them. They also are extremely sensitive when they get toward humans and so they're frequently hurt lots.

Pisces (Feb. 19- Mar. 20): This zodiac sign is enveloped in confusion and contradiction. Pisces is taken into consideration as "the saint and the sinner" within the zodiac. People born beneath this signal are often pressured which path they need to soak up life. They are the style trend-setters, they prefer arts and philosophy and a number of them are lost souls. Some people born below this signal are visionaries and majority of the arena-famous billionaires belong under this sign. On the alternative hand, majority of the human beings internal prison cells, reform establishments and rehabilitation center also belong to this Zodiac.

Pisceans susceptible point is their emotion that's why they constantly have to be cautious. This zodiac sign is divided into extremes where miracles and disillusionment show up. It is commonplace for Pisceans to be stuck up in their fantasies that they often miss out on the fact earlier than them. They see the world in unique mild. They see it how they need to look it and so whilst something takes place unexpectedly, they may be always caught off-shield.

Pisces is the maximum touchy sign the various zodiac. They are emotionally pushed. When they are in love, they may be usually on a cloud 9 but whilst they're harm, Pisceans turn out to be very depressed, harassed and obsessive. They cannot flow on without problems. It takes a long time and lots of excursion for them to recover from heartbreak.

Their creativeness is unmatched with the aid of any other zodiacs that's why Pisceans could make the great artists and storytellers. They are very perceptive. Extreme caution is wanted when entering a commitment with a Pisces. Even a simple and inconsiderate remark can hurt them deeply. They are genuinely onion-skinned so being tactless isn't always tolerable around them.

Chapter 4: Love Compatibility Of The 12

Zodiac Signs

I'm certain you need to recognise if you are like minded with your crush. Or perhaps you need to understand why you may't appear to apprehend different humans's temperaments. Well, in case you want to find your love match, it's the best region to be.

1. Aries:

Best Match: Aries is well suited with Leo, Libra and Sagittarius. But Leo is the correct in shape for the robust Aries. They each percentage a Fire sign and feature loads of things in common. Just beware because if one betrays the opposite they could actually explode.

Worst Match: Cancer can by no means move proper with Aries. They will generally tend to conflict all of the time. Aries dominant nature will certainly annoy the retrospective and moody Cancer.

2. Taurus:

Best Match:Ideal matches for Taurus are Scorpio, Leo, Virgo and Capricorn. The satisfactory fit may be Leo or Scorpio. Leos and Taureans are both bodily attractive which is essential for both of them. Leo wishes to expose off and so they will bathe the Taureans with lovely matters which Taurus will significantly appreciate. Both are unswerving symptoms so the relationship will genuinely ultimate. Scorpios then again will carry out the high-quality in a Taurean.

Worst Match:Gemini is just too restless for Taurus. Sagittarius care-unfastened persona will annoy the Taurus. Aries' sturdy character will conflict with the stubbornness of the Taurus until they work it out.

three. Gemini

Best Match:Libra is the pleasant in shape for Gemini. They have sufficient similarities and differences to make the relationship paintings. Other possible matches are Leo and Aquarius but courting with Leo is risky.

Worst fit: Cancer is greater domesticated and you are rarely domestic. Taurus is just too slow for you whilst Pisces is simply too sensitive that you'll harm them all too often.

four. Cancer:

Best Match:Cancer whilst paired with a fellow Cancer is a in shape made in heaven. But if no longer, Capricorn, Pisces and Scorpio could be a higher opportunity. Pisces is aware the depth of your emotions like no other.

Worst Match:Aries are too sturdy-headed for you and their dominant character will usually clash along with your devious facet. Geminis are out-going and also you're domesticated. Sagittarius is just too tough to address for you.

five. Leo:

Best Match: Aries is the fine suit for Leo due to the fact only Leo can tame the pinnacle-robust Aries however whilst one betrays the other, all hell breaks free for these signs and symptoms. Aquarius also can be an awesome suit for Aries for they may be without a doubt outgoing and cool. Sagittarius is likewise every other.

Worst suit:You can't last with a Gemini for they're ruled by their minds and you are along with your heart. Capricorns will now not tolerate your wants to overpower them and Pisces will be harm deeply by using you and they may not forgive you for that.

6. Virgo:

Best Match:Pisces is the perfect in shape for Virgos. Everyday might be thrilling for the two and they can conquer all limitations for their qualities supplement each different. Taurus is also an excellent match for you due to the fact they've a massive coronary heart and Capricorns may be notable commercial enterprise partners.

Worst match:Aquarius will by no means please you. You will continually be at every other's throat. Aries is too bossy and Libra is unable to stand your criticisms.

7. Libra:

Best Match:Aries is the ideal fit for you. You're both completely opposites however when it labored out it's miles a suit made in heaven. Aquarius is also an excellent candidate. You both love beauty and those in addition to Gemini.

Worst fit:Virgo and Scorpio is your worst match. They are too fussy and too serious in your colourful outlook.

8. Scorpio:

Best Match: Taurus is the first-rate healthy for Scorpios. Scorpios deliver out the satisfactory in Taurus and Taurus has a lot in commonplace with the Scorpios. The simplest hassle might be their jealous nature and possessive attitude however if each will work it out, this healthy is the most best match feasible. Cancer, Pisces and Virgo may also paintings properly with you.

Worst fit:Aries is the worst healthy for the Scorpios due to the fact each have the tendency to rule and simplest one may be the king of the family. Both are dominant and both will try to overpower each other leading to an everlasting conflict of the zodiac. You'll be jealous of Gemini's freedom and Sagittarius will bring out your worst traits.

nine. Sagittarius:

Best Match: Both Aries and Leo apprehend completely your temperament as Fire signal. They can tolerate your passion and pastimes. Gemini may be attractive but such enchantment will not final.

Worst Match:Capricorn is just too negative for you. Taurus is simply too possessive and you're a freedom-seeker. Virgo is simply too keen on criticisms which you cannot stand. Scorpio is as dominant as you so you will handiest clash. And Cancer is simply too domesticated at the same time as you're too out-going.

10. Capricorn:

Best Match:Taurus is a superb in shape due to the fact they are sweet and kind and they will encourage you to try tougher. Cancer is familiar with your tendency to be workaholic and could stability you with their advantageous qualities. Virgo is the ideal fit due to the fact they apprehend your perfectionist character and will paintings difficult with you to reach your desires.

Worst healthy:Leo is simply too outgoing so you cannot trust him that smooth. Aries is too impatient and dominant which negates your slow method to lifestyles. Gemini will no longer fee your ideals and Sagittarius is better off as an enemy.

11. Aquarius:

Best Match:Libra and Gemini are your best fits. They apprehend your on my own time and admire what you're fond of doing. Gemini loves adventures much like you and Libra appreciates your eye for sensuality and splendor.

Worst Match:Taurus is your worst in shape due to the fact you are too unstable for them. You live within the destiny even as Taurus lives inside the moment. You like modifications and Taurus hates it. Cancer is likewise not a great in shape due to the fact they may be too domesticated for you and Virgos are perfectionist so your disorganized attitude can in no way please a Virgo who is organized.

12. Pisces:

Best Match: Cancer or fellow Pisces may be the nice fit for you. Cancer knows your touchy nature and could help you. Virgo is your contrary zodiac however may be actually a terrific healthy when differences are worked out.

Worst suit:Leo will entice Pisces handiest to be forged apart later. Aries is simply too sturdy, harsh and aggressive on your sensitive and smooth nature. And Gemini will never be able to pay attention to your needs because they are easily distracted.

Money, Wealth and the 12 Zodiac Signs

Career, money and wealth are 3 matters people don't forget crucial to them. Money is good and important as lengthy as it's nicely utilized. But why do human beings make properly cash and others don't? Why is it that a few people achieve their chosen career while others don't? Well, every zodiac has its very own characteristics. Why force a herbal artist to become an unproductive legal professional? It doesn't make sense. Here is a guide for every zodiac signs and symptoms in terms of cash, wealth and career.

Aries:

Aries human beings love action. They are extremely competitive in fact they without difficulty lose interest without a opposition. They are usually on the flow and so after they have a job, they'll certainly excel while they may be given a hard activity. If they're running for a regulation organization, an Aries will shine if he's continuously within the midst of legal battles. He will now not sit and watch for the time to pass. Any subject activity is surely for Aries. He will now not be contented with just an excellent income. His paintings wishes to be very aggressive and difficult. Without a opposition, Aries people become bored and that they begin to get bored inside the job which they will finally fail to do. Most Aries humans will honestly go after money but they know that money is not the whole lot. They want a process that demanding situations them.

Taurus:

Taurus people are very patient so the best job for them is something that requires lengthy hours of awareness. Taurus humans can sit for long durations of time doing a sure challenge that captures their interest with none problem. They usually experience threatened by pressure. They are genuinely no longer the sort to be bossed around. They don't like to work for some thing that continuously demands their ingenuity. Security is very crucial to Taurus human beings. The enterprise has to actually be a solid employer for them to be virtually effective. They like to work within the sidelines. They carry out higher whilst they're in a supporting function. When it comes to money, Taurus is evidently fortunate. They are awesome in managing their cash however they can be impulsive buyers at times.

Gemini:

Gemini human beings are the 'talkers' of the zodiac. The pleasant process for them is some thing so that it will permit them to have interaction and talk to humans. It can be sales, survey, interviews, and customer service-orientated jobs, counseling jobs or sales. Gemini humans will really live to tell the tale a mundane and dull job however they'll sooner or later suffer intellectually and emotionally. It is continually essential for them to mingle with other people. They are clearly imaginative in terms of finishing a venture. They won't do a habitual job as it will bore them however they could make new approaches to make a ordinary process interesting sufficient for them, they simply have their very own way. When it comes to cash, Gemini humans are the excellent humans within the zodiac in making a living. They are evidently cash-makers. Their creativity in unequalled on the subject of making a living.

Cancer:

Cancer humans are moody by means of nature but they may be defensive of people and something they preserve critical to them. So, the satisfactory jobs for human beings born under this signal are instructors, medical doctors, nurses, or captain of the ship. Anything that requires them to think about different humans is a process so one can carry-out the real skills of a person born below the sign of Cancer. They also can be desirable chefs as they need to think of their customers while getting ready meals. Cancers are not affected by the outdoor forces of their job. The trouble is within them. Since they usually generally tend to exchange moods, Cancer human beings find it tough to cope with the changes in their careers. But after they discovered how to cope and manipulate their mood swings, they will absolutely outshine the relaxation of their area. Cancers are money-pushed. Money could be very critical to them and so they chase after it. They are generous to those critical to them so which can make up for their selfish streaks at times.

Leo:

Leos can be the most smug of the zodiac when their honor is taken-advantaged of. They want to be noticed and accolades or appreciation for his or her work is certainly a have to for a Leo. They aren't hungry for attention. They do no longer call for attention for not anything however due to the fact they believe they deserve it. Leos feel the need to paintings nicely as it's the simplest way they could do some thing tremendous. And they recognize more than each person else that while you do a incredible task, you can be observed. Most Leos excel in their process irrespective of what it is as long as it allows them to show-off their talents. They despise working in the sidelines and somebody else will take the credit. No, they may no longer tolerate it. Once their honor or their pride is overstepped by means of somebody, a Leo will show him what it's want to pass him over. He will now not remorse it although he loses

69

his task when his pleasure is extra important to him. When it comes to cash, Leos may be very beneficiant and lax. There are times whilst they are additionally very careless with their money and so they lose it unknowingly to a person else.

Virgo:

Virgos are not born-leaders. They do no longer enjoy the highlight. Instead they may be superb with agriculture and some thing that requires nurturing for boom. They have a strong experience of provider for others and so the quality jobs for Virgos are teachers, whatever associated with surveying, fishing and farming. They also can be exact docs or nurses as they're capable of nurture and care for their patients as they get properly. Since they're certainly meticulous, any task that requires precise precision and perfect timing is pleasant for a Virgo. They select the outdoors too. So they can be very first rate engineers or architects. When it comes to cash, they're no longer genuinely true in earning money because they are regularly shy and in order that they leave out a number of exact opportunities. But when they do have cash, they are able to handle it perfectly well way to their meticulous nature.

Libra:

Librans are diplomatic through nature and so any kind of task that requires diplomacy is nicely-perfect for them. They do no longer like being on the top spot as they hate pressure and first rate obligation. They might be glad and contented with just enough energy, an amazing associate, and a quiet and nice work environment. Librans get easily distracted and an excessive amount of closing dates and pressure will motive them to breaks down and depart the process almost right away. When they do attain the top spot, they need in reality succesful and superb assistants due to the fact they may be no longer good with selection-making. They want their assistants to supplement for what they may be missing so that it will excel. The first-rate jobs for Librans are anything associated with human aid and personnel branch, structure and the humanities.

Scorpio:

Power is extremely important to this zodiac signal. Scorpios always purpose to be the maximum powerful. Therefore, it is not sudden in any respect whilst a Scorpio rises to the top and holds the torch of electricity. Any management position is exceptional proper for a Scorpio. They have enormous management capabilities and they don't deserve a process that isn't always as challenging as they want it to be. They love a habitual and mundane task because it's far the form of task with a purpose to get them wondering on a each day foundation. The hassle with Scorpios is they're workaholics. When they immerse themselves in a specific job mainly the highbrow kind, they cannot effortlessly turn off their interest and consciousness even after paintings and so that they generally tend to get genuinely absorbed and overlook what it feels like to have a life in their personal outdoor the workplace.

Sagittarius:

People born under this sign are flexible and really energetic. They need constant change and once they don't they will sense stressed and forced and bored. Sagittarians love demanding situations. For them their career is a technique for them to ideal themselves and no longer only a necessity in existence to build up wealth. Career is a steady studying process for them and in order that they learn loads of factors as they attempt to satisfy their roles. The hassle with too independence and alternate is that they regularly change things for the sake of converting it. They often overlook the significance of other's evaluations because they truely want to trade it. The pleasant jobs for them are whatever that calls for steady innovation and creativeness. Anything associated with advertising, promotions, designs, style, and humanities are best suitable for them.

Capricorns:

Capricorns are quality suitable to take in top jobs. They are very realistic and so they make desirable selections useful to the corporation or the corporation. They are very disciplined and so they can work well notwithstanding many restrictions and they follow the rules with none lawsuits. They are not without problems intimidated. And they without a doubt work tough to attain their desires. Capricorns are very bookish and predictable because of their herbal admire for the norms. This is pretty a hassle whilst a activity calls for consistent imagination and innovation. They want ingenious and creative assistants or workforce while this happens in order that they may be a success. The high-quality jobs for Capricorns are some thing related to politics, neighborhood governance, and organising an corporation.

Aquarius:

Aquarius people are very original and individualistic. And so the great task for them is whatever so that it will provide them their very own area to do their own factor. An Aquarius works first-rate while he is on my own and no longer monitored. Not because they do no longer admire the guidelines and policies but due to the fact they genuinely need to be left on my own and do their personal component their personal manner. When they may be given a job, it is usually exceptional to allow them to do it on their own. When their boss is nosy and continuously telling them what to do, they will virtually now not do it in any respect. Aquarius people aren't exact group players. They will make suitable dentists, artists, and anything they are able to do by myself. They can be anticipated to produce fantastic effects when they're now not monitored. Their atypical way of doing their process makes them stand out. They don't want to waste their ruin-time doing some thing they don't assume is critical to them. They also are very resilient and which will work for long hours.

Pisces:

People born beneath this sign are very sacrificing and they don't care running for a touch pay so long as they discover what they're seeking out of their job. Pisces human beings are usually sensitive and shy and so they despise any form of activity that calls for them to stand out and meet the closing date. They want to be left alone when they paintings because consistent monitoring will cause them not anything but pressure. When they paintings without any stress, monitoring, or time limits they may be very efficient. They don't need to be compelled on doing something they're no longer inclined to do. They have a noble heart and so they continually attempt to do something for the common precise.

Chapter 5: Astrology And Elements

Future is indeterminate! Nobody is familiar with the happenings just after a few seconds! In truth absolutely everyone is aggravating approximately destiny and desires to recognise the prevalence, precautions & protection and treatments to live healthful and satisfied. For this, Astrology is the Key to open the beyond and prospects of hidden treasures and tragic of our existence.

Astrology emerged from 'astro' denoting 'stars' and 'trademarks' symbolizes 'language', collectively connotes the 'language of stars'. Astrology is the sacred and ancient technological know-how of concerning the maneuver of planets with the people and revealing their lifestyles.

What are the 4 elements?

Tradition perspectives the whole universe consisting of 4 elements that represents the basic trends and emphasis on horoscope. The emphasis or non-emphasis of factors within the person horoscope explores essential elements of character. The four factors of astrology seek advice from the vital energies that make up the complete advent comprehended via human beings.

The astrological birth chart starts offevolved from the primary breath of human beings. The factors inside the birth chart display the strength styles and vibratory manifestations. The mix of those elements on your start chart throws light on individual's nature and life classes.

The 4 elements which might be the primary ideas of lifestyles are—Fire, Earth, Air and Water. Each of the factors corresponds to a basic sort of power and recognition that operates inside all people.

Elements and Sign

According to the chronicles, 'Ptolemy' is ascribed in making the correlation among the 4 factors and the signs of astrology by assigning 3 zodiacal symptoms to every detail within the second century AD. The zodiacal wheel including twelve symptoms reflected the balance of four elements.

The character is strongly acquainted with the detail of any signal and includes cognizance and mode of belief for that reason. The elements of the signs are denoted by color. Fire that's purple shows spirit or identity, earth is inexperienced pronouncing practicality, air is determined black with intellectual & social topics and water that is blue specify emotions and soul.

Fire signs and symptoms

People are spontaneous, impulsive and practice their energies to its fullest. Their life principle is clear as enthusiasm, spirit, active, stimulated, faith, encouragement, self-expression, out-going, emotional and a energetic imagination.

Earth Signs

These people acts slowly, quietly and lightly because the response. They are sensual, grounded, and emotion-complete and have a tendency to exchange slowly. They are probably toward the bodily paperwork and are practical sufficient to enhance the material global via utilizing it.

Air signs and symptoms

They are highbrow, conceptual, and quick, lively and practice their energies in numerous methods. These are determined with mind's sensation, perception, thoughts and expression inside the non-public and social interplay.

Water Signs

These humans have empathy, cooling and healing sensitivity with others. They are quite creative, nurturing, introverted and deeply emotional rooted in their lives.

Elements and Modalities

To recognize the numerous patterns of forces is to evaluate them in phrases in their modalities. Each of the four factors have three modes in 3 vibrational modalities— Cardinal, constant and mutable. Cardinal denotes- Creative and active, Fixed represent-keeping and preserving, Mutable connotes-adaptive. Assimilating and synthesizing.

Cardinal Signs

These human beings are self-starters and doers. They represent the route of beginning moves of electricity and get matters step by step. However, people with few planets beneath this sign face hassle inside the quick of things.

Fixed Signs

These human beings sustain and maintain life. They syndicate the awareness of power amassed inwards closer to a center or radiating outwards from a middle. They are on the center of factors and resolutely refuse to go together with alternate. However, humans with few planets underneath this sign are quick of persevering and the capability to comply with through.

Mutable symptoms

These human beings are correlated with flexibility and steady trade. The human beings below these signs are adaptable, indecisive and transformative. They integrate, communicate and help matters to trade. Also, they're deeply receptive and affected by the surroundings. However, people with few planets might also face issues being bendy or adaptive to modifications.

Elements and Groups

Traditionally, elements are inform aside into companies—Fire & air, and water & earth. Fire and air are well-concept-out energetic and self-expressive. Whereas, water and earth are measured passive, receptive and self-containing.

This differentiation proves beneficial as an entire to the delivery charts as a way to make a distinction about the individual's energies and approach of self-expression as opposed to taking a huge view over the features of all of the humans indiscriminately in sure category.

Each sign of precise detail allude to numerous expressions, elemental strength, and ranges of development as well as the relationship of power. The zodiac signs categorised to every of those agencies of elements have the fact that signs and symptoms of the same element and detail within the equal organization have a choice of being well suited to every other.

Astrology and Signs
What are zodiac symptoms?

The signs and symptoms are the strength styles that syndicate precise and distinct characteristics of an man or woman. The zodiac is a circular belt of space within the heavens such as the manoeuver of orbits and planets along with the luminaries- sun and moon. The zodiacal circle is divided into twelve components and is called because the symptoms of zodiac.

The different planets of not like nature are continuously travelling thru the zodiacal circle thereby exerting an influence on the nature of signs and symptoms according their separate traits.

Fire signs- Aries, Leo, and Sagittarius

1. Aries (March 21 to April 20)

You are the primary signal of Zodiac. You are a born chief and shine bright in a crowd human beings. You take initiatives fearlessly in the whole thing and find out the unknown in lifestyles. You are lively, dynamic, active, courageous and fighter too.

You are impulsive, concentrated and spontaneous and often act first and think later about your movements & reactions. You are your very own boss and control your destiny. You are adventurous and appreciate independence of expression. You hate laziness and be given all the challenges with passion. Your finest strengths are self assurance, self-warranty and target-oriented. However, occasionally these strengths make you self-targeted.

Aries are interest-getting, competitive and competitive. Aries have the urge to 'Be'. If you can learn how to stability your staying power and sensitivity with boldness and determination, you may transform your lifestyles magically and you'll be plenty loved by means of your close to & expensive ones!

Symbol- The Ram, Ruling planet-Mars, House- 1, Number- 1, Gemstones- Diamond and opal

2. Leo (July 22 to August 23)

Sun, your ruling planet, is placed at centre and so is you- golden globe! You are dynamic, energetic, and generous and want the fine in existence. You urge to 'specific'. You are creative, expressive and feature delight and possession. You love to act, play, romance, kids and carrying.

Leo is dignified, dramatic, flamboyant, radiant, unswerving, joyous and playful. You are aggressive, confident and outgoing. You are true at expressing in theatres and arts. You have a big heart and love animals too.

Symbol- lion, ruling planet- sun, house- five, Number- five, gemstones- peridot, jade, sardonyx and diamond

3. Sagittarius (November 22 to December 21)

You search for fact, religion, philosophy, ideology and for the unknown things. You are bountifully enthusiastic, non secular, beneficiant, jovial and optimistic. You are profound, frank, expansive, aspiring, abstract, rich and humorous. You look for wisdom and are very direct & to the point. Sagittarians are appropriate natured, tolerant and magnanimous. You are constantly welcomed in politics and groups due to your philosophical and a ways-reaching energies.

Symbol- archer, ruling planet- Jupiter, house- nine, wide variety-nine, gemstone- lapis lazuli, turquoise and onyx.

Earth symptoms- Taurus, Virgo and Capricorn

4. Taurus (April 20 to May 21)
Taurus is ready having, responding and valuing. Taurus is steady, planned, decided and reaction to lifestyles's new ideas and impulses. These are fixed, sensible, strong, aesthetic, creative, methodical, sensual, dependable, retentive and private.

You search for pleasure, comfort and safety. You like to create and nurture physical kinds of splendor and produce forth boom and improvement. Taurus is mild, loyal, steadfast, decided, accepting, mothering and presents a base to possess and collect things.

Symbol- bull, ruling planet-venus, residence-2, wide variety-2, gem stones- emerald and sapphire

five. Virgo (August 23 to September 23)

These are involved with conservation, salvage, harvesting, repair and preservation. They are urged to serve and rules initiation and apprenticeship. Virgo is professional and is aware of using craftsmanship, equipment, evaluation, organisation and discrimination. These are busy, cautious, systematic, concerned, discerning, self-sacrificing, worrying and practical.

They love to serve. Ordering and organizing are the high attention of this signal. They are compassionate and responsive, martyr and frequently deal with others in place of themselves. They constantly need perfection.

Symbol-virgin, ruling planet-mercury, house-6, range-6, gemstones-sapphire, zircon and agate

6. Capricorn (December 21 to January 20)

Capricorns are worried with achieving the long term intention or plan. They are clear-seeing, sensible, formidable, disciplined, reserved, careful, skeptical, restrictive, sober, orderly, controlling, and manipulating. However, they are unemotional and un-tolerant. Capricorns are targeted on their career and reputation. Capricorns believe in difficult work and are logical.

They achieve mastery and success and tend to become improved and extra enjoyable with the passage of time and age.

Symbol-sea goat, ruling planet-Saturn, residence-10, number-10, gemstone- garnet and emerald

Air symptoms- Gemini, Libra and Aquarius

7. Gemini

They have an infinite search for enjoy, expertise, limits and limitations. They like to be in movement, speaking, inquiring, investigating and exploring. They are often apprehensive, versatile, resourceful, curious, changeful, quick, reasoning. Gemini seems to examine and talk.

They like to make connections via letters, phones, speech, mind, writing and mental processes. Gemini is verbal, mental and stressed, impartial.

Symbol-twins, ruling planet-mercury, residence-three, range-3, gems-alexandrite, agate and amethyst

8. Libra (September 23 to October 23)

It always surrounds marriage and partnership. It seeks stability and concord. It specializes in the principle of unconditional attractiveness or reaction. They are diplomatic, compassionate, attentive, appreciative, appealing, cooperative, thoughtful, compromising.

They want union, reconciliation and balance. It dreams for romance and splendor. They are god-talented artists, mediators and facilitators, peace makers, sensible and communicative. They do not like coarseness and social gracious. However, while faced any undertaking proves 'iron fist in velvet glove'.

Symbol-scale, ruling planet-venus, residence-7, range-7, gem stones- opal, sapphire and jasper

9. Aquarius (January 20 to February 18)

They deliver the religious light of ideals into fact. Aquarius is impersonal, inclined to paintings with everyone protecting same aspirations. They like crew work. Aquarius is aspiring, innovative, individualistic, futuristic, eccentric, rebellious, humane and idealistic.

They are looking for to go beyond, freedom and equality. They characterize humanitarian dreams, idealism and altruism. Aquarius is always non-partial and non-sectarian. They recognition on such dreams which can be nice to many humans. They price individualism, freedom and equality. Aquarius are innovative, intuitive, discoverer and unconventional and genius too!

Symbol-water bearer, ruling planet-Uranus, residence-eleven, range-11, gemstone-amethyst and bloodstone

Water symptoms- most cancers, Scorpio and Pisces
10. Cancer (June 21 to July 22)

Cancer is homesick humans and likes to be t house or home. They are emotional, protecting, domestic, sympathetic, responsive, structured, caring, moody, supportive, and comfortable.

Cancer is the mom of zodiac defensive and providing for others. They are sensitive and emotionally bonded in relationships. They are searching for emotions, agree with, protection, consolation and nurturance.

Symbol-crab, ruling planet-moon, residence-4, wide variety-four, gem stones-ruby, pearl and moonstone

eleven. Scorpio (October 23 to November 22)

They searching for transformation, changes in marriages or union, sharing of assets, emotions and intimacy and the modifications made by using those sharing. Scorpio desires elimination and purification via doing away with the extra. They are penetrating, purging, powerful, compulsive, intimate, ecstatic and cathartic.

They are encouraged with the aid of electricity. Scorpio is passionate, excessive, magnetic, charismatic and private. However, they're found secretive approximately private feelings. They are excessively possessive and jealous and face problem in letting go. They want non secular nature or socio-political electricity.

Symbol-scorpion or phoenix, ruling planet-Pluto, residence-8, quantity-eight, gemstone-topaz, pearl, citrine

12. Pisces (February 18 to march 21)

They searching for to surrender. Pisces is compassionate, susceptible and intuitive. They are a nature of consider, ingenious, receptive, mysterious, mystical, psychic, stimulated, vague, elusive and knows sacrifice. They get the inducement from cohesion, inner truth, and values.

They are deeply rooted to spiritual and mental. Pisces is very understanding, patient and lengthy-suffering. They regularly misunderstood the things. They are kind hearted and forgive effortlessly. They are without difficulty moved by way of the emotions of surrounding human beings and are escapist!

Symbol-fishes, ruling planet- Neptune, residence-12, quantity-12, gemstone-bloodstone and jade

Astrology and Planets
What are planets?

Planets are the heavenly bodies that control the glide of power and constitute the elements of enjoy. Moon, Mercury, Venus, Sun, Mars, Jupiter, Saturn, Uranus, Neptune and Pluto.

In astrology, those ten planets are considered according to their length, proximity and affect on the planet and thereby, to the humans, animals and count!   Each of the planets has its own particular personality, power, functions and susceptibilities.

The planets are essential to take a look at for the creation of start chart. The sun and moon (planets in astrology) are essential heavenly bodies found in each chart. At new moon, it's far said that we start, build, expand and acquire new things and strength.

Sun

The solar tells us the internal self and spirit of a person. It exhibits to us the overall vivacity and ability to claim one-self. Its urge is to 'BE'. It is a mentor or embodiment of authority to which all of us appears up and gets. The sun is an enlightenment and perception of our-selves as a sovereign character and the center and initiator of very own truth. It desires to be famend and to specific them-selves.

Moon

The moon is referred to as the mom of planets deeply rooted with emotions and choice to generate security inside the international. It feels an urge to inner maintain up, domestic and emotional safety. Moon needs emotional concord and a experience of belongingness. It influences our mobility, flexibility and flexibility to alternate.

Mercury

The mercury has conscious, rational and logical thoughts. They represent an urge to specific the reviews and intellect thru ability and speech. They represent verbal exchange and setting up connections and relationships with others. Mercury is the messenger of God and thus, reality. It needs to analyze and express verbally the ideas and thoughts by means of being reasonable.

Venus

What are planets?
Planets are the heavenly our bodies that manage the flow of energy and represent the elements of revel in. Moon, Mercury, Venus, Sun, Mars, Jupiter,

Saturn, Uranus, Neptune and Pluto   In astrology, those ten planets are considered in line with their size, proximity and have an effect on on the planet and thereby, to the people, animals and remember!   Each of the planets has its very own specific character, electricity, functions and susceptibilities. The planets are important to examine for the introduction of start chart. The solar and moon (planets in astrology) are critical heavenly bodies found in every chart. At new moon, it's miles stated that we start, build, expand and acquire new matters and power.

Sun

The solar tells us the internal self and spirit of someone. It well-knownshows to us the general vivacity and ability to assert one-self. Its urge is to 'BE'. It is a mentor or embodiment of authority to which anybody seems up and gets. The solar is an enlightenment and insight of our-selves as a sovereign character and the middle and initiator of very own reality. It needs to be famend and to explicit them-selves.

Moon

The moon is called the mom of planets deeply rooted with feelings and desire to generate security within the world. It feels an urge to internal maintain up, domestic and emotional protection. Moon wishes emotional concord and a experience of belongingness. It influences our mobility, flexibility and adaptableness to change.

Mercury

The mercury has aware, rational and logical mind. They constitute an urge to express the critiques and mind thru ability and speech. They characterize verbal exchange and establishing connections and relationships with others. Mercury is the messenger of God and for this reason, reality. It desires to examine and express verbally the ideas and mind with the aid of being reasonable.

Venus

Venus symbolizes love, sharing, cherishing, sensuality, enchantment, concord, grace, beauty and compassion. Venus is responsible for seeking splendor to your existence, sharing with pals and lovers, nourishing artwork, innovative eloquence and music on your soul. It has an urge for being societal and love, fondness and happiness. It needs soothe and harmony and desire to be close to others.

Mars

Mars represents ardour, strength, braveness, willpower, dedication, spontaneity and pressure of someone to explore and journey new experiences. Mars are impulsive to take actions and aggressions. They have an urge to act undoubtedly, self-confident, and competitive. They need to accomplish their requirements and wishes bodily and sexual satisfaction.

Jupiter

Jupiter represents the existence course, the way thru, continuity and succession. Jupiter symbolizes direction finder, desirable fortune, success and good fortune. It illuminates and guides via knowledge while there's darkness in existence due to Saturn. Jupiter constantly grows and seeks journey. It searches for religion, consider and self assurance in life.

Saturn

Saturn syndicates ethical conviction and sense of right and wrong. It symbolizes the powers of fortitude and the capacity to pay attention and create structures that serve our highest prospective. It outlines maturity, area, top efforts and properly use of resources. It has an urge toward protection and protection thru sizeable fulfillment. It teaches obligation, willpower and perseverance.

Uranus

It specializes in individualistic freedom and independence from self-ego and esteem. It has an urge in the direction of delineation, creativity and reliance from culture. It desires alternate, exhilaration and expression without strength of mind. It stands for instinct, proposal and insights. It is a extremely good awakener and inventor and seeks liberation.

Neptune

Neptune is the dissolver of restrictions. It is kindhearted, sensitive, holy and the manual and non secular mom. It seeks for agree with and religion and lay down arms to the typical anonymity of harmony. It has an urge to break faraway from the boundaries of 1's self and the cloth global. It symbolizes loose-will and union.

Pluto

Pluto has an urge in the direction of general renaissance and penetrates to the foundation of enjoy. It symbolizes self-refine and needs to permit cross of antique plans. It searches for transformation, transmutation and removal. Pluto shows how we compact with strength, private and non-non-public anguishes. Pluto is the lord of underworld-loss of life and rebirth.

Other Celestial Bodies
Besides those planets, astrologers pay attention to the several different heavenly our bodies like asteroids- Chiron, Ceres, Pallas, Juno and Vesta that have an impact on with a minor impact to the people. In Our solar device, planets revolve round solar inside the identical path but some of the planets are visible transferring backwards occasionally. This retrograde movement of planets is likewise studied by way of the Astrologers.

Mars

Mars represents passion, strength, braveness, dedication, willpower, spontaneity and power of a person to explore and adventure new reports. Mars are impulsive to take moves and aggressions. They have an urge to behave positively, self-assured, and competitive. They want to accomplish their necessities and desires physical and sexual satisfaction.

Jupiter

Jupiter represents the lifestyles direction, the manner through, continuity and succession. Jupiter symbolizes course finder, right fortune, achievement and success. It illuminates and publications through information while there's darkness in existence due to Saturn. Jupiter usually grows and seeks journey. It searches for faith, agree with and self assurance in existence.

Saturn

Saturn syndicates ethical conviction and judgment of right and wrong. It symbolizes the powers of fortitude and the ability to pay attention and create systems that serve our maximum prospective. It outlines adulthood, field, precise efforts and right use of sources. It has an urge in the direction of protection and protection thru considerable fulfillment. It teaches duty, self-discipline and perseverance.

Uranus

It specializes in individualistic freedom and independence from self-ego and esteem. It has an urge in the direction of delineation, creativity and reliance from tradition. It desires exchange, exhilaration and expression without strength of mind. It stands for intuition, thought and insights. It is a brilliant awakener and inventor and seeks liberation.

Neptune
Neptune is the dissolver of restrictions. It is kindhearted, touchy, holy and the guide and non secular mother. It seeks for consider and religion and lay down arms to the general anonymity of unity. It has an urge to break faraway from the limits of one's self and the cloth international. It symbolizes free-will and union.

Pluto

Pluto has an urge toward total renaissance and penetrates to the inspiration of revel in. It symbolizes self-refine and wishes to permit move of antique plans. It searches for transformation, transmutation and elimination. Pluto shows how we compact with electricity, private and non-non-public anguishes. Pluto is the lord of underworld-death and rebirth.

Other Celestial Bodies

Besides those planets, astrologers pay attention to the numerous different heavenly bodies like asteroids- Chiron, Ceres, Pallas, Juno and Vesta that impact with a minor effect to the human beings. In Our sun gadget, planets revolve round sun inside the equal direction but a number of the planets are seen moving backwards sometimes. This retrograde movement of planets is likewise studied by way of the Astrologers.

Astrology and The House

What is house gadget?

The astrological house demonstrates us which spheres of lifestyles obtain more weight than others in a horoscope. Each astrological house stands for a specific section. The house division of a horoscope contrasts from individual to individual as it is measured according to the time of start and the geographic function of the place of start.

The horizon- Ascendant and Descendant

This axis that divides the horoscope into an higher and a lower half of symbolizes the horizon at the time of beginning. The factor at which the eastern horizon traverses the ecliptic is called the ascendant.

Planets found near the ascendant at the moment of beginning are rising. It is the commencement or cusp of the primary house. On the alternative hand, the descendant is observed at the cusp of the 7th residence. The planets close to the descendant are placing.

The Meridian- imum coeli and medium coeli

The different huge axis in house division is the meridian. This split the horoscope into an japanese and a western 1/2. The maximum point of juncture of this axis with the ecliptic is called the Medium Coeli or mid heaven. Planets close to to the Medium coeli live within the maximum viable region in the heavens on the time of delivery.

The decrease point underneath the horizon is known as the Imum Coeli. The planets near the imum coeli reside within the lower aspect of the earth.

1st House

The signal at the beginning of the primary residence notify us approximately someone's qualities, temper and foundation. It symbolizes our interpretations, immediately, inborn response and demonstrates how we constitute ourselves to the sector.

second House

The 2d residence revolves round verbal exchange and its inhabitant enlightens us approximately the fabric instances, the grasping urge and how we % with possessions and materialistic approaches. This embraces the relationship to our personal frame.

third House

The 1/3 residence and the planets concerned tell us of our siblings and the mode in which we speak on an on a each day foundation level and the relationships which determine our regular life.

4th House

This residence depicts our origins, the parental domestic and the state of affairs persuading formative years and youngsters. It describes how we speak to family, our mind-set towards father, heart and domestic.

5th House

Sexuality and eroticism are at 5th house, along side all styles of creative appearance. This residence also portrays how we relate to kids, delight and fun in lifestyles.

6th House

The 6th residence illustrates the situations neighboring us in our daily lives, which includes the work environment and daily practice. This includes our deeds toward subordinate humans. Physical hygiene and care also feel right here, as well as dispositions to sure acquired sickness.

seventh House

The descendant signal and planets regarding the 7th house inform us approximately how we select our soul-associates and explain the partnerships and relationships we look for.
8th House

The eighth residence gives you an concept about how we narrate to communal items and the way we cope with material loss. Traditional astrology continues that this house has an affinity to demise and all matters metaphysical. Death could then be the closing fabric loss and the study of metaphysics can be a very distinguish manner of dealing with this loss.

ninth House
The ninth house describes our religious leaning, existence philosophy and our international outlook. These are often prejudiced through journeys to foreign international locations. The attitudes cultured and shaped in this residence can greatly sway topics of the tenth residence.

10th House

This residence is of specific importance because it influences our preference of profession and our experience of calling. This maintains at some stage in our lives. According to custom, and experiences, this residence expresses the relationship with mother.

eleventh House

The eleventh house describes how we relate to friends, supporters and mentors. This residence shows how we communicate about the society in which we live to tell the tale.

12th House

This house represents the ones levels of life in which the character no longer plays a part, wherein we step again for a higher whole. Astrology sees hospitals, prisons and psychiatric establishments on this house. It is also related to monasteries.

Astrology and Aspects

What are Aspects?

The full of life connections between the various energies of life are represented on the individuals with the aid of the elements in a natal or beginning chart. These components are the angular distances among the planets in a horoscope, measured as angles within ecliptic circle.

These interactions impact the running of planets together. Aspects are the strains of pressure amid various strength centers, planets, in energy fields recorded by means of the chart. The factors are calculated within the 360 ranges circle, revealing the electricity fields inside the birth chart. Aspect amongst planets creates both easiness and is considered as presents or frictions which might be placed up in challenges to conquer.

Aspects and Groups

Aspects are classified in organizations.

Disharmonious or hard components

As the call suggests, the disharmonious components creates terrible consequences and strain in lifestyles. It refers to the main elements that are opposition (180 tiers), square (ninety stages), and minor factors encompass grand pass, quincunx (a hundred and fifty degrees).

Harmonious Aspects

As the call shows, the harmonious elements are taken into consideration advanced. It refers back to the trine (one hundred twenty levels) and sextile (60 stages) which are the major factors. The minor elements includes quintile (72), bi-quintile (one hundred forty four), semi-sextile (30 degrees).

Major Aspects

Opposition (a hundred and eighty stages)

This foremost thing is regarded as disharmonious or dynamic. It has a encouraging and revitalizing effect. The high-quality of the element relies upon at the planets caught up. As a whole, an opposition caught between two planets creates anxiety amongst them with fine results.

Square (90 tiers)

The square is regarded as a disharmonious thing because the planets implicated look like blocked. The tribulations that take area from the rectangular preserve on turning bad. The complexity lies in trying to bring collectively forces which can be looking to circulate in absolutely diverse directions. As a rule, this takes the form of desires and requires which can be similarly confined.

Trine (one hundred twenty tiers)

The Trine is a harmonious element wherein the planets effort collectively in a gracious way via enriching every different. Trine give you an concept about where your natural talents lie and it relies upon on you in what way you make use of your competencies. The planets in Trine assist every different. They allow you to be given others, your self and the instances.

Sextile (60 degrees)

The Sextile have a harmonious impact that definitely depends on the planets involved. Sextile also explores your abilities and ease like the trines however, trines come very naturally to the people while sextile are very overt to the native. Sextile are outgoing and courting-pleasant components. They divulge the ability and skills for sensible use of energies.

Conjunction (zero tiers)

The conjunction is a harmonious component and depends on the planets concerned and how near the element is. Planets and points that define a conjunction are energies which are unified. They are merged and proceed together. For instance, if the space among mercury and solar becomes less than a few ranges then mercury will burn! As an entire, conjunctions display an instantaneous relationship that works in one way or any other.

Minor Aspects

Quintile (seventy two stages)

The quintile tends to be a harmonious however minor thing in which planets involved are at a distance of seventy two tiers. The planetary energies connect you to your internal and outer self by using the use of your inherited capacities and insights, termed as religious astrology.

Bi-Quintile (one hundred forty four tiers)

A bi-quintile is a minor and harmonious thing to intellectual place, in which planets concerned are at a distance of 144 levels that's double the quintile thing. This helps you to stride into master consciousness and acknowledge your latent potential for mastery.

Semi-sextile (30 stages)

The semi-sextile is a harmonious minor aspect in which planets concerned are at a distance of 30 stages and has a less impact than a sextile. The planetary energies are associated however they influence each other obliquely.

It can specific a lack of ease and can manipulate the improvement of your welfare. It has the capability to make you aware of your innate persona.

Grand Cross

The grand move is a disharmonious issue where planets are located at 90 stages apart. It is the most entrenched and steady pattern, giving exceptional sensual, practical, and psychic perception. The universe revolves round a stable structure. It can be a basis of electricity and firmness, however additionally may also have a tendency to be self-defeating because of the push for moving into a number of instructions at once, thereby getting into no direction.

Quincunx (one hundred fifty ranges)

The Quincunx is a disharmonious and minor thing in which concerned planets are one hundred fifty degrees aside. This aspect implies a need for adjustment or a trade of approach. The planets involved share nothing in not unusual, so it's far a totally hard element to integrate into our being. The only way of changing the disharmony of this element is to reliance one's internal voice in order that you could move in advance into transformation and incorporation.

Astrology and Horoscopes

What is the distinction among Astrology and Horoscope?

Horoscope is simply a blue-print of your moves, a delivery chart or natal chart that consists of interpreted matters approximately your-self. On the alternative hand, Astrology is a 'technological know-how of stars' that obtrusive itself thru studying, reading, knowledge and interpreting the horoscope.

What is Horoscope?

The word horoscope has emerged from Greek words 'Hora' and 'scopos' connoting 'time' 'observer'. The horoscope is an astrological chart or diagram that corresponds to the positions of the sun, moon, planets, astrological components and prone angles at the time of an prevalence like the delivery of a person. The other names of horoscope are- Natal chart, radix, sky-map, cosmogram and so forth.

A horoscope is said to be an astrologer's interpretations based at the planets and solar signs and symptoms. Although, there is no clinical proof of the accuracy of horoscopes and the strategies utilized in putting interpretations are nicely concept-out pseudo-medical. To put together a horoscope, 3 kinds of records are required- Date of Birth, time of beginning and area of beginning.

What horoscope enlightens you?

In our life, we learn a plethora of subjects on various subjects- mathematics and technological know-how, literature and languages, geography and history, arts and many other subjects in colleges and universities. However, we aren't taught tons approximately ourselves and each different that could lead to a happy and enjoyable life ahead. To know ourselves we want to examine horoscopes! It doesn't promise to forecast your future incidents but it reveals your private traits that what form of character you're.

A lot many human beings lives inside just one person. Sometimes you sense cheerful however now and again you are sad and need to be left on my own. Sometimes you are critical & considerate and now and again you crave amusing! These variegated facets of you're the signs and symptoms of sun, Moon and planets at your beginning to make you stay for your exceptional with those various visage.

The horoscope gives you an idea about the fantastic connection among the Sun, Moon and planets at the time and vicinity of your beginning. A horoscope channelizes you to discover the right direction of your existence by showing the points of interest of your capabilities, conscious, feelings and the things that satisfaction you.

Personalities through Planets

• The Sun depicts our goals for the deepest aspirations in life.
• The Moon tells us our emotional values and emotions.

- The Mercury exhibits how we assume and specific ourselves.
- The Venus shows our relationships and communications with others.
- The Mars represents our capability to make use of our electricity and skills in attaining our desires.
- The Jupiter gives an concept of our enjoyment and know-how.
- The Saturn illuminates our willpower and power of person we've in ourselves.
- The Uranus demonstrates our creativity, inventive, naturalist and originality.
- The Neptune explains our assisting conduct to others that how we assist every other.
- The Pluto makes us recognize the ways we will grow thru intensifying our self-understanding.

How Horoscopes Work?

The horoscopes function a map of heavens inclusive of interpretations which are calculated to forecast the personalities of each person. Horoscopes are designed and planned in accordance with a few principles – Native, celestial sphere, aircraft of the equator, plane of the ecliptic, plane of the horizon, angles, homes, zodiac signs, placement of planets, and aspects. These additives are already defined in the previous chapters in detail.

Health, Career,and Marriage Through Astrology

Health and Astrology

'A sound mind is living in a valid body'. Health is named as best whilst every organ of the body in addition to mind works powerfully with out sickness and harm. For a nourishing and precise fitness, the surroundings in which we live performs a essential role. According to Astrology, all the stages of life of a individual are managed via the twelve houses, such as fitness. Each of the twelve houses represents our frame organs and the horrific effect of malefic planets on those twelve houses creates health problems for that specific organ.

Houses and Diseases

- First residence: Mind, face, head, appearance and complexion, general health, lengthy existence and cranium.
- Second House: Right eye, throat, neck, teeth, mouth, gums, gullet and larynx.
- Third residence: ears, hands, fingers, shoulders, proper ear and nerves.
- Fourth house: breasts, chest, lungs, belly, elbow joint.
- Fifth residence: stomach, heart. Body electricity, backbone, liver, Spleen.
- Sixth residence: digestive device, kidney, massive gut, colon, uterus and anus.
- Seventh residence: glands, renal device, buttocks, adrenals and personal elements.
- Eighth residence: scortum, pelvis, seminal vesicles, intercourse organs, venereal diseases, ovaries, prostate gland.
- Ninth house: hips, thighs, knees, joints, bones, hairs and returned.
- Tenth house: knees, joints and bones.
- Eleventh house: calves, left ear, left arm, move, legs, enamel, ankle.
- Twelfth residence: left eye, lymphatic gadget, feet, tooth.

Depression and Stress

Today, pressure and melancholy have emerge as commonplace problems in everybody's lives. It becomes a extreme count number if depression strikes you often and holds you in its grip. According to Astrology, despair and stress is brought on due to the malefic outcomes of planets on homes.

The first, ascendant, suggests mind and the manner our mind thinks and react. The wrong placement of ascendant and the awful thing of malefic planets create strain and state of melancholy in life.

The fourth residence is for mental peace, happiness and luxury. If the fourth house is faulty, then it is void of strength and creates a demanding and depressive life.

Also, moon necessitates our lifestyles with emotions. If moon is developing awful outcomes within the sixth, eighth and 12th residence, conjunction of moon with malefic planets, Saturn factors moon, hemming of moon among two malefic planets, and moon posited with solar are the motives for melancholy and pressure.

Astrological treatments for health & depression issues

Gemstones are represented as powerful weapons towards the susceptible planets to gain and enhance health problems in lifestyles. Each planet has a gem stone consistent with shade that attracts the cosmic power of that specific planet. In primordial length, gem stones have been worn by way of kings in crowns with a faith of wealth, prosperity and protection from malefic planets.

Gems in addition to the ashes of gem stones are used to deal with various illnesses. Gems are appealing, metaphysical, optical, recuperation and cosmic remedy to provide strength t the vulnerable planets. But, do not forget, gemstones ought to be worn via consulting an skilled and knowledgeable astrologer.

• Blue Sapphire: Help in curing Bone and knee problems, rheumatism, paralysis, madness, lack of electricity.

• Red Coral: Help in curing acidity, indigestion, stomachs, fever, small pox, lack of energy, piles, boils, and measles.

- Ruby: Help in curing bones, blood strain, coronary heart troubles, rheumatic pains, loss of self assurance, risky mind, and bad eyesight.
- Pearl: Help in curing wrong sleep, depression, madness, susceptible mind, indigestion, asthma, tuberculosis, coronary heart troubles, menstrual disorders and vulnerable eyesight.
- Diamond: Helps in curing urinary problems, susceptible uterus, diabetes, weak reproductive organs, sexual relationships and urinary tract contamination.
- Emerald: Helps in curing asthma, madness, mental ailment, epilepsy, susceptible thoughts, stomach problems, gastritis, pancreatic issues and insomnia.
- Hessonite: Helps in curing bronchial asthma, madness, intellectual ailment, obsessive issues, epilepsy, susceptible mind, belly troubles, leprosy, insomnia and other illnesses that are hard to diagnose.
- Cat's eye: Helps in avoiding mishaps, mystery enemies and accidents. It treatment options obsessions, insanity, mental issues, urinary issues, paralyses and belly troubles.

• Yellow Sapphire: It enables in curing liver and kidney troubles, gouts, jaundice, hernia, obesity, rheumatism and heart issues.

Career and Astrology

Today, a number of people are lagging behind in their vibrant future and profession. In spite of owning an amazing training, competencies and qualification, maximum of the aspirants fail to get activity. Astrology says that choice of accurate profession is the most issue you have to do. Astrology enables in locating the right choice of profession for people with a view to gather an ideal profession. The study of planets, Astrology helps in getting task in addition to promotions in jobs for people who are already in activity.

Houses and Career

Each House has its own significance in the profession. The planet suggests the best career for a shiny profession that should be considered by means of the man or woman. You can study the zodiac signs and symptoms (chapter 2) for understanding approximately your features, career and powers. The placement of sturdy planets in numerous houses represents the correct profession.

• First house: It suggests success in discipline of self-employment.

• Second house: It shows profession in banking, investments, finance, coaching, experts, writing and publishing.

• Third house: It denotes conversation, advertising and marketing, salesmanship, advertising and marketing, pc, internet designing, journeying, writing and import-export.

• Fourth house: It represents land and automobiles, agriculture, constructing, sale and purchase of motors, mining.

• Fifth residence: It explains advertising, brokers, finance, education.

• Sixth house: It syndicates loan, police, litigation, livelihood, court docket, loan-restoration, clinics.

• Seventh residence: enterprise and partnership, buying and selling.

• Eight house: Insurance, studies, astrology, magical powers.

• Ninth house: It represents success and religion. Career consists of law, priest, head of religious frame, and tour to non secular locations.

- Tenth House: Career includes government jobs, politicians.
- Eleventh house: all planets right here deliver top outcomes. It represents profits from various assets.
- Twelfth residence: foreign nations, import & export, journey enterprise, hospitals, prisons.
-

Remedies to enhance profession

In astrology, Saturn necessitates importance in profession and professional lifestyles. It gives problems in lifestyles in addition to within the profession. If the Saturn is laced wrong for your chart, such issues will occur. But, don't be dishearten as Saturn causes only put off and hurdles, no longer denial. Saturn is a remarkable mentor that makes you understand from the difficulties and disasters. It is the Saturn which has the capacity to present everything back in future.

The tenth lord performs an critical position in making a really perfect career. Tenth lord in Ascendant shows self employment, in 2nd house it guarantees profession in coaching and banking area. The tenth lord in 0.33

residence syndicates communication, publishing and computer discipline. Its presence in 4th house represents actual property commercial enterprise, agriculture and mining. The 10th lord in fifth residence indicates funding in inventory market, criminal advisors and army quarter. Its performs a amazing position within the seventh residence by using showing fulfillment in partnership.

The tenth lord in 8 residence depicts research as profession and ninth house as pilgrimage, tours, professors and lecturers in institutes. Its presence in the tenth residence promises process in authorities officers and control fields. The 10th lord in eleventh residence shows profession associated with finance or trade and 12th residence as scientific and foreign career.

Thus, the lord of 10th house ought to be made sturdy to obtain success in career and profession. For the achievement in employment as promotions, blessings of Lord Saturn must be taken to gain victory. The people who are trying to find profession in lawyer, politics and academic institute need to make the Jupiter robust to achieve triumph.

On the alternative hand, preserve scenery of mountains or hilly area on back facet of seat in the places of work. In respective of all of the professions, your seat need to in no way be under a beam. Never face without delay towards wall even as you are sitting in a chair. It emits effective strength and effective results on your career.

Marriage and Astrology

Marriage has always been a situation for all individuals who doesn't get a existence partner or a suitable fit. Ages passes and some of the human beings get disadvantaged of the wedding and its happiness.

Today, marriage has turn out to be a difficult part for the eligible character and mother and father too due to the increasing training and knowledge and expectancies in existence. The existence is tons complicated and aggressive that makes delay in marriages. Moreover, the wedding charts do no longer in shape and due to the non-compatibility again, issues occur in fixing a marriage.

Love marriages

It is constantly favored to seek advice from an astrologer and to fit the horoscope charts earlier than fixing a marriage. Besides, within the gift situation, love marriages are getting popularity and recognition global.

Astrology says that love and romance is indicated when Venus is in union with the Ascendant and is laced with 5th, seventh or eleventh residence. Astrologically, 5th house in horoscope suggests love and romance. Seventh house belongs to partner and the relation between the 7th and 5th house effects in love marriage.

In love marriages, change of lords and factor of benefice Jupiter makes the love marriages strong. However, the lack of faith, divorce is the results of malefic Rahu, Mars or Saturn bringing disharmony and breaking of relations.

Remedies for successful marriages

- An auspicious end result will emerge if benefic planets are located in 7th residence. If malefic planets are located within the seventh residence then it will be an inauspicious situation for marriage and hence, put off in marriages will arise.
- Saturn plays a primary function in delaying the wedding.
- Harmony and bliss may be visible if the lord of 7th house aspects its personal residence.
- If malefic planets are located within the 8 residence of horoscope, durability of spouse suffers and so healthy making must be accomplished with warning.
- Jupiter gives bliss of marriage in particular homes in horoscope.
- Mars performs an vital position in giving happiness and harmony in marriages. If Mars is positioned in first, fourth, 7th, 8th or 12th residence of horoscope, it is not an auspicious healthy and have to be taken out carefully.
- The role of planets in tenth and 0.33 residence represents right or terrible relationship with the in-legal guidelines and brother-sister-in-legal guidelines.

• After consulting the astrologer, gems ought to be worn to make robust your vulnerable planets related to seventh residence so that you can get fulfillment in marriage.

Chapter 6: The Air Symptoms – Gemini, Libra

& Aquarius

In this chapter, you may study:
The symbols, stones, and ruling planets of the air symptoms
What each zodiac signal method
How they may be prompted through their planets
Why they're given their symbols

Gemini - May 22 - June 21
Symbol: The Twins
Ruling Planet: Mercury
Stone: Aquamarine
The ruler of Gemini is Mercury, which in Greek mythology was the gods' messenger. Therefore, Geminis are usually looking to acquire more understanding and new reports. They are very curious and love range, that's why they are inquisitive about basically everything. They will test and attempt most things and are continually on the flow looking for something new.
The Twins of the zodiac have a habit of talking quite a lot all of the time, and if they're no

longer speaking, then they're writing or otherwise taking an hobby inside the linguistic elements for which they've unique skills. People are frequently talking approximately them, exactly because they've such "huge" personalities and are such interesting people. Some might even say they're gossiped about, because the speak is not usually right.

Positive: Geminis entice cash, accurate fortune, and interesting studies anywhere they cross. They don't take life or themselves too critically and that allows them hold a fairly care-free mind-set.

Negative: Because they live such comparatively disorganized lives, if we have been to take other signs into attention, their non-public subjects regularly occur to move awry. Romantic relationships, specially, aren't always a success.

Libra - September 24 - October 23
Symbol: The Scales
Ruling planet: Venus
Stone: Opal

Libra is dominated through Venus and, as its image shows, is the most balanced sign inside the zodiac. Libra requires this balance of their lives which will be capable of exist in concord with the people around them and with themselves. Generally, they are the humans trying to ensure that everybody is content and glad – this is one among their defining traits. When their loved ones are satisfied, Libra is glad. Most people don't know, however Libra is a piece of a dreamer. They tend to be idealistic at times, dreaming approximately their ideal love and attaining romantic perfection.

But they don't handiest dream, although – they work closer to making their desires come real. They will work hard, but in addition they want to keep that sensitive balance among their private lifestyles and their expert one. The importance of this cannot be hyped up, due to the fact Libra relies upon on this feel of equilibrium with a view to keep their emotional lifestyles in take a look at.

Positive: Libra cares deeply for the humans around them and will constantly attempt to make each person happy. They are extremely fair people – equity and justice are very vital to them.

Negative: Because of this tendency to place others first and make every person else satisfied, they will turn out to be self-sacrificing for the sake of others. Their tendency for taking a long time to make decisions doesn't continually replicate kindly on them, both.

Aquarius - January 21 - February 19

Symbol: The Water Bearer

Ruling planet: Uranus

Stone: Amethyst

The image for this sign, dominated by means of Uranus, is the water bearer. This guy carrying a pitcher of water is the only to represent Aquarius, due to their function generosity, each with their material possessions and their time. They are continually supporting someone else and are always involved in a few humanitarian attempt or some other. They "carry" people on their backs or they "convey" assets to assist them. One way or another, they work tough in the direction of being of carrier to the people round them, who would possibly find themselves in need.

This signal is almost always misplaced in deep idea and their thoughts is usually racing, seeking out new ideas. They like to invent new things and come up with innovations, this means that they may appear like emotionally eliminated, however they are simply busy wondering. Their robust tendency towards highbrow knowledge makes them born leaders, trailblazers, and average, very specific people. They don't follow the herd, so to speak, however act on their personal accord and are often trendsetters.

Positive: They in reality have a thoughts in their very own and can be very innovative and modern individuals. You received't see them following traits, due to the fact they may be those who set them, inside the first vicinity.

Negative: Because of their propensity for deep concept and seemingly impassive existence, they could sometimes get lost of their personal inner global and emerge as dour or even depressed.

Check your understanding!

Can you call one effective trait and one negative trait for each air sign listed here? Think of someone you recognize who shares one of the air signs – do you recognize any of their trends right here? Name some.

The Water signs – Cancer, Scorpio & Pisces
In this bankruptcy, you will learn:
The symbols, stones, and ruling planets of the water signs and symptoms
What each zodiac signal means
How they may be motivated with the aid of their planets

Why they are given their symbols

Cancer - June 22 - July 22
Symbol: The Crab
Ruling planet: The Moon
Stone: Moonstone
Cancers are under the guideline of the Moon, which makes them very mysterious people. Some might say they may be veritable enigmas, as they seem like very contradictory in nature. They are frequently very perplexing to the people round them, exactly due to those temper swings and unexpected changes, from one intense to the opposite. This may be visible as eccentric, mysterious and exciting, however no longer all of the signs can be so type whilst judging Cancer's conduct.

The reason for the numerous changes that Cancer goes thru is the ever-changing Moon. The Moon actions via one-of-a-kind stages, which means Cancer is at once motivated via it and could exchange in conjunction with it. "Moon Children" can be hard to apprehend, unless you have gained insight into their external, astrological affects that permeate so strongly into their regular lifestyles.

Positive: Despite their changing behavior, Cancer isn't always flaky. On the opposite, this signal may be very reliable and is a actually appropriate pal. They are extraordinary in helping their cherished ones and are very devoted to their own family.

Negative: As I referred to earlier, the sudden and frequent modifications in temper aren't appreciated by means of all, and can make Cancer seem a bit scatter-brained and unstable. They are normally lovely people, but they are able to get extremely jealous, that can emerge as a real hassle.

Scorpio - October 24 - November 22

Symbol: The Scorpion

Ruling planet: Pluto

Stone: Topaz

Ruled by way of Pluto, Scorpio is assumed to be an antique soul and the very best power of the complete zodiac. They tend to be very smart people, and their lives are frequently awesome and dramatic, mainly with regards to non-public relationships. Scorpios are, indeed, very clever and informed, and seem like the keepers of all of the answers. Scorpios are very passionate individuals and love performs a big role in their lives, but they're additionally electricity-hungry and this quest for electricity often competes with their choice for love.

Scorpio's symbol, the scorpion, turned into now not selected at random. The animal demonstrates among the equal traits as humans born in Scorpio, such as the reality that they are not aggressive, until provoked. A Scorpio will never "sting" you out in their own accord, however they will absolutely reply to provocation.

Positive: Scorpio loves to win and that they frequently do, because they're one of the effective, winning symptoms. Because they've such an imposing character that demands interest and appreciate, they're often deferred to.

Negative: They have a tendency to cover from those around them and no one ever is aware of what they may be questioning or feeling. This can specifically impact intimate partners, who can stay for years with a Scorpio, without ever understanding their true shades, emotions, or thoughts.

Pisces - February 20- March 20
Symbol: The Fish
Ruling Planet: Neptune
Stone: Bloodstone

The fish is a fitting symbol for this sign, because it represents fluidity, in addition to mystery and secrets and techniques. Pisces leads a totally active indoors lifestyles that is in no way too obvious at the outside. They are deep thinkers and the closing daydreamers of the zodiac. They also are the maximum sensitive signal of the twelve, so that you may also need to be careful around them.

One fundamental factor about Pisces is they want to see every person round them content material and happy. It sincerely influences them deeply when the humans they love are unhappy, and they'll usually try to make certain all of us is in excessive spirits. In their non-public relationships, they may be unswerving and dedicated and will continue to be constant for years at a time, for they do now not like change or switching partners very often. This is likewise proper for their expert life, wherein they are similarly unswerving employees.

Positive: Pisces also can show amazing ardour in all elements in their lives, whether it is the creative endeavors they may be so talented at or in their romantic life.

Negative: One of the maximum not unusual and obvious shortcomings of Pisces is that they worry so much. They can make themselves ill through worrying over the smallest things, however don't have a tendency to proportion their mind with others, which could purpose disconnection with their intimate companions.

Check your understanding!
Which is the most touchy sign of the zodiac?
Why is Scorpio's image so suitable?

The Earth signs and symptoms – Taurus, Virgo & Capricorn

you may examine:
The symbols, stones, and ruling planets of the earth signs and symptoms
What each zodiac signal means
How they may be inspired by their planets
Why they are given their symbols

Taurus - April 21 - May 21
Symbol: The Bull
Ruling planet: Venus
Stone: Emerald
Taurus is represented by way of the Bull and dominated via Venus, and as such, they're very calm folks that tend to preserve to

themselves. It's now not that they do now not socialize – they're really excellent at it – however they don't stay with the group. Taurus is very gathered or even methodical, just like the bull. However, they do thoroughly experience luxury and take delight in all its paperwork, whether it's intercourse, food, or cloth possessions.

Because of their peaceful demeanor, Taurus isn't always brief to anger, but once they do attain that point, all and sundry else had higher be careful, due to the fact this signal is risky. Much just like the bull, while Taurus receives angry, all they see is crimson and they'll absolutely act upon it. This sign is understood to be absolutely in touch with their senses, and that they generally love the whole thing that has to do with the bodily thing.

Positive: They are unbiased individuals and don't keep that many human beings round them for the simple truth that they don't want them. They feature so well on their personal, that they don't experience the want for all and sundry else's help or companionship.

Negative: Because of their solitary nature, Taurus can appear dull, withdrawn, or be visible as a snob. They don't allow others to see the fact in their personality, so very few human beings get to sincerely recognize them.

Virgo - August 22 - September 23
Symbol: The Virgin
Ruling planet: Mercury
Stone: Sapphire
Virgo is represented by way of the Virgin or the Maiden, due to how calm and accrued it's miles. This signal knows the way to maintain their cool demeanor and manners, but on the interior, they are bursting with thoughts and interest. Virgo is one of these symptoms whose thoughts is usually active and who by no means ceases to suppose, to create, to invent, and analyze. They are gifted and creative spirits and take fantastic pleasure in producing and developing splendor.

In addition, Virgo is understood to be very nurturing and that they love taking care of others or catering to their needs. Consequently, their career is regularly linked with serving, assisting, or looking after others – they may be docs, nurses, instructors, social people, and so on.

Positive: Virgo is stuffed to the brim with empathy and that they do truly sense awful when their loved-ones are depressing. They can't stand to look people struggling, that's why they are trying to help and generally tend to select careers in aiding others, as nicely.

Negative: Because they are so kind and so eager to assist others, they're frequently taken benefit of or harm with the aid of the human beings around them, who see them as weak. The truth that they're quiet individuals doesn't help with that, both.

Capricorn - December 23 - January 20
Symbol: The Goat
Ruling planet: Saturn
Stone: Garnet
Capricorns, symbolized through the goat and dominated by way of Saturn, are sincerely of two distinct types. First, there may be the extremely bold Capricorn, represented with the aid of the mountain goat. This Capricorn won't stop till they meet their dreams. On the flip facet, there's the so-known as garden goat, which is the relatively extra reserved Capricorn. Not as formidable in spirit, they are content with much less and won't project into new grounds unless they actually ought to.

But no matter the sort, Capricorns are very severe, quiet resilient creatures. They are extremely hard working and very reliable. They make splendid friends and dependable companions, whether or not in commercial enterprise or love. This signal is one which you could anticipate, irrespective of what and they may do everything in their energy now not to assist you to down. Capricorn is affected person, accountable, and an overachiever.

Positive: Capricorn is one of the maximum dependable signs and symptoms within the zodiac, no matter if it's paintings or love. They put their coronary heart into some thing they do and are extremely dedicated. This can become a trouble in terms of paintings, because they lose the stability among work and play.

Negative: Capricorn is the very definition of the workaholic. Thoroughly in love with their work, and borderline captivated with reaching their goals, this sign can sometimes get so carried away, that they lose the line delimiting their expert life from their private one.

Check your understanding!

Do you observed the bull is the ideal symbol for Taurus? Why?

What is the distinction among the 2 special forms of Capricorn?

The Fire signs – Aries, Leo & Sagittarius
you may learn:

About the symbols, stones, and ruling planets of the fireplace signs

What each zodiac signal way

How they're encouraged by way of their planets

Why they're given their symbols

Aries - March 21 - April 20

Symbol: The Ram

Ruling planet: Mars

Stone: Diamond

Staying real to its identity as a hearth sign, Aries, represented by means of the Ram and ruled through Mars, is an adventurous sign. They are impartial and outgoing and are acknowledged to stay children at heart. They can seem very assured and mature, however they are secretly very naive and harmless. Aries hold a unique mixture of trends, for it is also one of the very resilient signs and symptoms.

In the alternative sex, Aries seems for characteristics that will supplement and support them. Masculine men and feminine girls are the best companions for Aries of each sexes, because together, they acquire crowning glory. It can be hard for Aries to find their different 1/2, because they're so particular. They gift both female and masculine developments, in order that they want different things from a considerable different.

Positive: This signal loves a mission and they will take it fortuitously. They experience operating hard to triumph over them, and show that they may be capable. That's why they journey so much and tend to place themselves in unusual situations.

Negative: Aries is impulsive and rarely takes the time to assume earlier than they act. Naturally, this can land them into trouble extra often than they'd like, however it's miles in their adventurous nature that they can not deny.

Leo - July 23 -August 21
Symbol: The Lion
Ruling planet: The Sun
Stone: Peridot

Appropriately represented with the aid of the Lion and dominated with the aid of the Sun, Leos are fierce leaders and protectors. They have a disturbing presence and have a tendency to be in fee, whether at domestic or at paintings, because of their innate leadership capabilities and natural tendency towards heading operations. After all, the lion is the king of the jungle and this is sincerely apparent in Leo's attitude.

Leo is extremely attached to their own family and could do something to defend it. Not one to stray or search for steady variety, they will be loyal to their partner, kids, and loved-ones and could bathe them with anything they want, whether or not it's money, love, or safety.

Positive: People who percentage this signal have a keen sense of justice, no longer in contrast to Libra and will always try to do the right issue, consisting of status up for others and of path, themselves, when they sense that an injustice has been made.

Negative: Leo may be smug, and that isn't always just the impression that other human beings have of them. They can look like overly confident or too proud of themselves and their abilities and that can be off-placing for others.

Sagittarius - November 23 - December 22
Symbol: The Archer
Ruling planet: Jupiter
Stone: Turquoise
Sagittarius receives their excellent ardour for life from their ruling planet, Jupiter, that is their benefactor. This is one of the greater adventurous symptoms of the zodiac, continually on the circulate and seeking out their next new enjoy. They have a herbal inclination toward travelling and coming across new places and those and they can even lead a nomadic existence. That explains the symbol of the Archer, or the Centaur. In mythology, the centaur shot the bow and the centaur followed anywhere the arrow landed, so as to retrieve it and shoot it once more.

This sign is thought to be very intelligent and hungry for understanding. That is one of the reasons why they love travelling so much. This way, they can continuously research new things, meet human beings, listen to their tales and absorb as a great deal know-how as they can, before moving on to the next new location, wherein new facts and new studies watch for them.

Positive: Sagittarius is extraordinarily positive and firmly believes that something is possible, if they need it sufficient and work closer to making it manifest, whether or not it's far a professional aim or a personal one.

Negative: One of the pitfalls of this sign is precisely their optimism, that may grow to be delusion and be very detrimental to their evolution and nicely-being. Optimism is splendid, but being overconfident of their success and abilities can result in unlucky conditions.

Check your expertise!

Can you list a few trends that make Leos similar to their representative, the lion?

Why is it problematic for Aries to find a suitable romantic associate with a purpose to fulfill all their wishes?

Best Practices and Common Mistakes

Do's

Take this statistics as a chance to analyze greater approximately yourself. Your zodiac sign can suggest very thrilling factors of your personality, a number of which you won't even have been aware about.

Consider comparing what you're analyzing with what you recognize about your friends. As you examine approximately every signal, think about the people on your lifestyles which you understand who share that specific sign.

Be open to finding out new matters or converting your opinion on astrology and the zodiac. Unless you pass into it with an open mind, you gained't get very good consequences. Being open to discovering yourself and others, and maybe even transforming the way you look at other human beings is genuinely vital when studying approximately the zodiac signs.

Don'ts

Don't be judgmental of folks that practice astrology and those who trust in zodiacs. It's fine if you don't want to live your life consistent with the zodiac, however make a factor of no longer judging folks that do.

Don't allow what you recognize about the zodiac signs and symptoms prevent you from getting to know greater or unique facts. We gain extra understanding throughout our lives and what you already know can without a doubt be challenged!

Don't assume this expertise to rule your complete lifestyles. I've said this earlier than, but the zodiac will now not manipulate your existence. It can't show you the future and you cannot construct your complete existence around it.

Chapter 7: Aries - "Fight And To Be The Primary"

Influence: Mars
Symbols: ram, deer
Colors: scarlet, crimson, orange, mild brown, golden
Stones: ruby, purple coral, all styles of pink stones, diamond
Metal: iron
Talismans: Golden Fleece, Diamond
Happy days: Tuesday, Sunday
Unsuccessful days: Friday, Saturday
From March 21 to March 31: natures are born in particular brave, competitive, hard, robust, undisciplined, brave, are ardent in love
From April 1 to April 20: natures are proud, generous, noble, brave, capable of command, formidable, in a position to triumph over limitations, love for them is a excellent affection.

HEALTH

High blood pressure, furunculosis, lung and throat illnesses, injuries because of violence, fires and war. Also the vulnerable a part of the body - the head, the brain, the face, eyes, ears, tongue, teeth, nose, oral hollow space, top jaw, chin.

Parents of the kid Aries - should make certain that once analyzing is good lights, check whether or not glasses are wished, specially at some stage in puberty, that is on Aries because of inherent this symptoms of early intercourse power. Aries generally tend to carefree approximately their fitness.

Often these are reckless mother and father. They are hooked on everything that involves their thoughts, can exhaust themselves to exhaustion, which leads to accelerated stress, insomnia, creates susceptibility to coronary heart assaults.

The body of Aries needs constant schooling to avoid premature getting older, which for this sign is more normal than for others.

CHARACTER

Since Aries is a fireplace sign, its main function is pastime, willpower, directness, self-sufficiency, independence. Aries energy is an abrupt, robust stress inside the starting, whilst it ignites, there may be something new, but if the momentum is misplaced – it both fizzles out or it becomes not thrilling, now not in a position to finish the process. He wishes fans who can follow him and embody what he wants. He is a commander, who leads with him, is the leader. He is prepared to rush into any new event, if most effective he is not disturbed, prepared to guide.

People of this sign do not adore it when they're prevented. He is ready to demolish all boundaries, therefore he may be hard, aggressive, because what might not turn out to be he has to win and go ahead. Always goes only in that course that he himself chose, not taking note of no one. Very sincere, cannot maneuver. Strive for reality, for justice. It's a winner, a leader, a pioneer, the man in advance of all. Representatives of this signal can rush into various adventures.

In the highbrow sphere - quickly understands the essence of things, is logical enough, grasps everything on the fly, learns without problems (if fascinated). Is interested by something new, he studies even as it is thrilling to look at. Wranglers, can guard any point of view, iron good judgment, can argue every body.

Positive trends of character: clinical wondering, common sense, delight, self-confidence, restlessness of spirit, willpower, braveness, virility, bravery, prowess, insistence, perseverance, initiative, enterprise, extremely good punching strength, optimism, enthusiasm.

Negative man or woman traits: brief irritability, excitability, brief mood, impulsiveness, intolerance, stubbornness, quarrelsomeness, recklessness, an inclination to diverse styles of exaggerations and sensations, unbridled passions, aggressiveness, despotism, tyranny.

WHAT TO GIFT?

Aries is a sign of Fire, a person who loves the entirety vivid and beautiful. A top gift for a man Aries could be an ashtray, a lighter or other souvenirs associated with the hearth. Do not pick a present in black and white, grey, such things are not likely to love Aries. Also, they'll gladly receive such uncommon provides, for you to raise the mood, and convey new impressions - for instance, helicopter flight, a parachute jump certificates, a fitness card, and so forth. For a girl Aries - brilliant rings will fit, additionally a great present a fixed of fashionable jewelry with semiprecious stones, a lovely pen or a hard and fast of cosmetics. But in case you nonetheless have not determined what gift to make, you can ask Aries what he would love to get. Aries will only please this, so that you get a listing of the favored presentation.

FEAR - loss of cherished ones

Aries is ambitious and decisive, all of the actions he plays are really fearless. He has confidence that he can do something. Aries are very magnanimous and honest, they're strong in soul and body. They are very communicative, a good way to frequently be haunted by the concern of final on my own. Only the lack of loved ones or pals can scare Aries extra than defeat in conflict. Although they understand this most effective in reality, due to the fact they do not absolutely fail. Aries - self-confident and stubborn, don't forget their opinion to be the only accurate one, so they are angry whilst their judgments come to be wondered.

PROFESSION

Aries generally recognise their profession from youth or from school. Routine or sedentary work is an flawed preference. Can have a business and paintings for lease. Conflict, does now not listen to others, thinking about his opinion just like the most correct.

From Aries there may be a dynamic succesful sellers, touring salesmen, dentists, veterinarians, squaddies, policemen, butchers, superb mechanics, hairdressers, chefs, surgeons, sculptors. Get along well with fire and metal. Can be excellent athletes. Regardless of the selection of career, Aries aspires to be the first, the first-rate fighter. Aries is a younger sign, he desires a show-off.

MONEY

Aries is a chance sign and in this connection, its representatives are often worried in adventures associated with money, and from a younger age. Aries are considered the favorites of finance, and they reciprocate. This isn't unexpected. They are enterprising, willing to stick to an active existence function in all existence spheres, because of which, this signal of the zodiac regularly has enormous cash, and with them the Aries are now not forgiven for the rest of their lives. In the score of the richest and maximum a hit signs and symptoms of the zodiac - they occupy an honorable fourth place and might correctly name themselves the maximum inextinguishable millionaires.

LOVE

Ready for romance and intercourse at an early age. They tend at every age to fall in love at the beginning sight. If they fall in love, nothing will stand before their ardour. They are often interested in the forbidden fruit, they are searching for to get it at any value. In return, they're equipped to offer themselves. They are generous, from time to time prudent. With repulsion, Aries' ardour is going into obsession. Early pride and fury. On the opposite hand, they speedy try on and calm down.

For Aries, any stunning journey, temptations - an invite to trade. All Aries are impulsive, impetuous, sometimes naive. Fall in love easily, can get depressed, emotional, involved, even capable of get unwell, but a refresher new love can repair existence.

Always want some thing new. He does now not want to go through. He reveals it tough to cope while he is deserted. At the first sign of repeatability the entirety is thrown and removed. Touching enthusiasts, whose whims need to be happy just like a capricious child's. As kids they prefer to expose off and "pluck" applause. In a man there's some thing that ostentatious, and girls like to illustrate their blessings. They can be deeply dedicated, but temporarily, whilst relations are uncertain. Aries does now not tolerate being restrained inside the pursuit of the desire.

SEXUALITY

Aries is a completely passionate, active and energetic lover in bed. He can act fairly selfishly, but he knows how to make it in order that it is no longer only appropriate for him, however additionally for his accomplice. Sexual strength and the power of Aries can best be envied.

COUNTRY

In historic instances it become Aries who patronized Sparta. Spartans had almost all functions folks who had been born underneath the sign of Aries - militancy, purposefulness and asceticism. The current embodiment of Sparta have become - Germany. Of path, this doesn't suggest that every one Aries urgently need to p.C. Their suitcases and move to triumph over a brand new Motherland. But as an alternative for excursion, this country is still worth considering.

TAURUS - "To construct and to shield"
Influence: Venus
Symbols: winged ox, cow winged
Colors: crimson, translucent, lemon yellow, white, mottled, shiny
Stones: diamond, quartz crystal
Metal: copper
Talismans: owl, golden calf
Happy days: Friday
Unsuccessful days: Tuesday
From April 21 to May eleven: dreamy, noble, indecisive
From May 12 to May 21: unsociable, pessimistic, afraid of poverty and love loneliness

HEALTH

They are born with a robust charter and may reach old age without any sickness. A big deliver of vitality and energy. Taurus does no longer recognize wherein and when to prevent, is willing to paintings too much, drink, smoke, love. When he is unwell, too lengthy does not get better. Most illnesses because of excessive, often reason despondency. Weak locations of the frame: pores and skin, throat, ovaries, veins, kidneys, reproductive device, chin. He does now not want to exercising, weight loss program, physical strain and any restriction.

CHARACTER

The maximum sensual sign, very a great deal strives for beauty and superb, has aestheticism, a experience of shape and a choice for beauty. Sensitive and material signal, in phrases of nice and beauty. Taurus is "heat" and affectionate, deep, reliable, proper, concord in relationships may be very vital for him. At first he's calm, however if the cup of persistence overflows, it could emerge as explosive, hysterical, a typhoon of feelings sweeps the whole thing on its manner. At first, you can't circulate him from the area, and then you will now not be capable of "forestall" him. Very dramatize the state of affairs, apprehensive alertness. A dependable cloth rear is very essential. He does now not like to rush, the arena of dreams is the maximum important for him. Strongly cussed, if you begin to positioned stress on him, you may best influence Taurus with caress and persuasion. In research he chooses best what he likes, what he likes.

Positive developments: perseverance, perseverance, endurance, staying power, restraint, strength of will, ability to concentrate, consistency, honesty, decency, goodwill, conscientiousness.

Negative character traits: stubbornness, obstinacy, pessimism, laziness, apathy, slowness, conservatism, excessive adherence to subculture and entrenched rules.

WHAT TO GIFT?

Taurus likes to give classy presents, to indulge their loved ones with something exquisite. Of path, the identical in response, and they want from others. As a gift, all the classical ideas approximately the present may be suitable - a massive field of candies, pricey cognac, fashion bag, watch, decor for the residence, a practical cell phone of the today's version, or cash in an envelope, will suit you. Taurus is one of the maximum sensual signs of the zodiac. So you can effectively gift him a certificate for a rubdown within the spa. Clothing for Taurus deliver soft or silk, blankets - woolen and relaxed. Woolen scarves might be also high-quality present. All those products will no longer be best in pleasure, but will also calm the frightened gadget of Taurus. Taurus has a strong culinary alternatives and could gladly accept your present in the form of a scrumptious cake. Be positive to % it in a pleasing paper, with beautiful bows. Taurus can be touched via such diligence out of your facet.

FEAR - financial instability

Taurus is a calm, welcoming and pleasant sign of the zodiac, however he isn't always absolutely found out to anyone. To recognize honestly close him can best close household and friends, simplest to them he completely opens his sights and emotions. Taurus is stingy on feelings. The fundamental issue in life is domestic and own family fireplace, he prefers coziness, comfort, tranquility and tries to avoid scandals and quarrels. Considering the reality that Taurus desires comfort, they need to have a few economic balance, they cope with their cash very cautiously and do not recognize debts. Taurus does no longer save money just for the sake of accumulation, they shop money to spend. Nothing scares Taurus greater than instability - be it monetary or every other.

PROFESSION

In their youth they suppose lots about selecting a profession, they want to ensure that they may do all well and they will be capable of do the whole lot nicely, earn plenty. They do no longer item to ordinary, towards a certain repeatability that creates the affect of stability. They are committed to the policies and love achievement. The satisfactory use of Taurus is the entirety that provides reward, feel gratification - from farming to flower breeding, livestock, cook dinner, bakery, restaurant enterprise (the famous Chefs mainly Taurus).

Well manifests itself in acting: artists, doctors, masseurs, beauticians, selling high-priced and bohemian matters, song, portray, poetry, making a song, theater and cinema, display business.

MONEY

Representatives of this sign not often revel in acute economic want and deprivation. They do now not muddle the cash, spend it usefully for themselves. Some of them flip the earning and amassing cloth sources into the principle goal. Therefore, Taurus, typically, live in abundance, and plenty of even in luxurious. "People Taurus" want to cry about their economic state of affairs. This is because they may be now not darlings of fortune. To enhance their welfare they should exert effort and just a few Taurus can end up absolutely wealthy.

LOVE

Fall in love with "Love" long earlier than the advent of the primary lover. When this happens, they need time to awaken, open up truth, some other individual, till their persona will now not will become the item of affection. Passion even in greater mature years does now not get up unexpectedly, but grows slowly and imperceptibly, however whilst emotions are sunburned, there's no greater sensual signal. From his desire he does no longer back off.

For Taurus, emotions and desires are the identical. Their passion is full: it is going to the stop, no matter whether or not this stop is nice or sour. In love of Taurus, neither complaint, nor inconvenience, nor pain can prevent him, although in different respects Taurus is practical.

The sensuality of Taurus is better than the sexual act, it's far visible in the whole lot that relates to a loved one: garments, colour, scent, tone of voice. Love of Taurus conceals in itself the intimacy and isolation of the desolate tract island within the sunshine, the mysticism of a heat and dark cave. It is deeply touching, gentle, no longer complicated through anything and lasts a long time.

For Taurus, the old skool, romantic promise of eternal fidelity, dying like Romeo and Juliet keeps the pressure, if they intervene to their love, and that is inherent in younger and mature Taurus, both women and men. They need to personal the object of their love and belong to them to the stop. If truth does no longer correspond to the ideal, Taurus passes via the hell of jealousy, despondency, does no longer need any reconciliation and distractions, on occasion even can die because of a broken heart. They can fall into other extremes - "Don Juanism", alcoholism, gluttony, however this is tremendously uncommon. If Taurus overcomes his jealous strings, there's no greater perfect lover.

From Taurus will get gentle, warm parents, worrying for their children with pride. Taurus thrive in the harmony of circle of relatives life, do now not bear quarrels, can be slightly dictators in relation to kids.

SEXUALITY

Taurus loves and appreciates all carnal pleasures, whether it's delicious food, candy sleep or right intercourse. In mattress, as in lifestyles, he's inherent in thoroughness: possibly he can't be referred to as a temperamental lover, but he is aware of precisely the way to enjoy himself and supply it to his accomplice. His caresses - this is not a rush onslaught, however as a substitute a protracted love marathon. He has nowhere to rush, which include in bed: attentive and chronic, he is aware of the way to kindle a fire of goals in his partner and is determined to revel in it to the fullest.

COUNTRY

For Taurus, the international locations with saturated nature - Bulgaria - could be the most favorable. Taurus is an earth sign; peoples who live within the signal of "Taurus" nations respect the warm temperature and comfort of the home - including Japan and Switzerland, Estonia and Finland, Tibet and Australia.

GEMINI - "To invent and to talk"
Influence: Mercury
Symbols: winged truncheon
Colors: green
Stones: inexperienced emerald or jadeite
Metal: mercury
Talismans: snake, masks
Happy days: Wednesday, Sunday
Unsuccessful days: Thursday
From May 22 to June 10: may be aggressive, restless
From June eleven to June 21: overbearing, irritable, talkative, vain

HEALTH
The have an impact on of Mercury can cause intellectual, speech disorders, all styles of mental troubles, neuroses, neuralgia,

deafness, eye issues, dizziness, respiratory illnesses (trachea, bronchi, lungs, specially the higher part of the lungs and pleura), hand issues (fractures). Avoid high consumption of meat. Twins are often prone to insomnia, so that they do no longer relaxation well at night time. Despite all of the goal motives, they must be able to relax a good way to prevent nervous tension and viable worried breakdowns.

To save you illnesses, Gemini must monitor their fitness, extra regularly go to the clean air and take air and sun baths. If Gemini neglects such advice, it is able to badly affect their fragile health. Gemini get sick primarily not from overwork, but as an alternative from boredom and loneliness.

CHARACTER

Gemini do not tolerate loneliness and experience in a society like a fish in water. They without difficulty get acquainted, and hopefully stick with absolutely everyone - from public figures to drooping drunks. Gemini are likable due to the fact they get along a number of opposites, all sense them as their non secular brothers.

Alive, agile, talkative, someone with whom nowhere uninteresting, smooth on the rise. He likes to speak, he constantly finds something to talk about, has many friends, likes trips, tours. Gemini has a quick-witted thoughts, they fast understand information, are capable of capture the that means of what become said on the fly, has properly advanced good judgment, eloquence, there are usually many thoughts and plans that the fact is not always found out.

To the advanced thoughts have to be added painful sensuality, impermanence and a tendency to magnify trifles. They are unbalanced, inconsistent, do numerous matters at once, but are practical, sensitive. Gemini via nature are mild and variable. They are inner intellectuals. They have a changeable temper, they easily hold close everything, adore controversy and a laugh, have the ability to stay a twin existence.

Positive tendencies of person: a successful combination of intelligence and instinct, appropriate belief, quick response, mobility, observance, rich imagination and active, vibrant imagination, encyclopedic thoughts, interest, honesty, choose and goodwill.

Negative man or woman developments: frivolity, superficiality, variability, unreliability, windy, conceited, talkative, bloodless, rash in choices and deeds.

WHAT TO GIFT?
If you need to pick out the right gift for Gemini, you want to take into account a few functions in their nature. Gemini like new exciting information, that's why an amazing gift for them might be a new e book, mobile smartphone, with a minimum tariff plan, CD-disc to the laptop, the essential software program, an internet digital camera or pc, a subscription to the mag. If you have got some problems in what your Gemini is involved, you best need to ask him approximately his hobbies, and he'll solution you with a pleasure and enthusiasm about them, because it's excited by him. They like travelling, new impressions, so that the whole lot related to motion may be enormously liked by Gemini - it is able to be a thermos, snoozing bag, backpack, camp package. You even can gift to him a journey out of the metropolis for the weekend, and it'll be a first-rate gift.
FEAR – you decide

Gemini - a complex and contradictory signal, the maximum unstable and changeable of all the signs of the zodiac. The temper of Gemini is changeable because the weather: they may be thrown from giggling to crying, from like to hate, from pleasure to unhappiness. They can alternate their selections, choice — review their views or even take again their promises that they have got given each to themselves and to other. This nice in their man or woman makes them a skilled manipulators. They can alternate their opinion so regularly that you could effortlessly forget about about what they've stated in the beginning. But each medal always has two aspects and in this situation, the inclination to trade their choices is worry, or alternatively - fear of creating selections.

PROFESSION

Under the signal of Gemini many people of intellectual work are born. They opt for such paintings this is related with a continuous change of impressions and sports: advertising retailers, managers, tv and radio workers. They can work like: lectors, writers, speakers, economic workers, businessmen, journalists, astrologers, satirists.

Gemini have skillful in the languages that's why there are plenty of polyglots amongst them. Speech capabilities are so extremely good and sundry that they could persuade all people and in whatever. In their mouths, the maximum absurd thoughts sound reasonable, and the lie seems real.

MONEY

People who're born below this sign can easily earn cash. A lot of Gemini make money from the "air", succeeding within the records sphere and inventory transactions. If you distribute all the international's wealth on the signs of the zodiac, then the share of Gemini could have a strong part of them. But far no longer every Gemini can store the cash. If any coin appears at their hands, they have got a sturdy feeling to spend it. This is the golden mean, there's money, and the relaxation is each person's deal.

LOVE

As a rule the feelings of Gemini are mild and cellular, they are communicative and really charming, can seduce a word. They are amorous and clean to reply to courtship, do not thoughts to flirt. They do no longer like deeply immersed in emotion, can effortlessly smash off the connection. Easily transfer from one love item to any other. They do not like to discover the connection.

Gemini, almost always, marry more than as soon as, despite the fact that if the primary marriage is concluded later, the greater the likelihood that it will closing for a long time, maybe for continually.

SEXUALITY

Gemini hates ordinary and adore the whole lot new. This absolutely applies to their conduct inside the intimate sphere. In lifestyles, they are able to have many extra or less lengthy passions, as much as partners for one night, and sometimes they're able to twist two love affairs simultaneously. They do not have a excessive sexuality, but their partner isn't always going to be bored in mattress, Gemini are set up to test. They regularly reference to the e book for a while it is the Kama Sutra – as a minimum till then, till they try in it nearly all. However, in love, and in marriage Gemini are seeking out in a associate, in the first vicinity, not sexual, however highbrow compatibility.

COUNTRY

As for the country, which is ruled by this sign, to start with the US comes to thoughts. Here Mercury - the planet of Gemini - expressed itself maximum absolutely: in enterprise and trade, within the capacity to perceive and use the new, in a consistent readiness for change. It is curious that frequently the pinnacle of state reflects the signal or maybe the factors of his human beings. From current US presidents there have been Gemini: John Kennedy, George Bush, Donald Trump.

CANCER - "The vision and schooling"
Influence: Moon
Symbols: cancer, crab, claws
Colors: white milky, silvery, light colorations
Stones: pearls, moonstone
Metal: silver
Talismans: Clover
Happy days: Monday, Thursday

Unsuccessful days: Tuesday, Saturday

From June 22 to July eleven: frivolous, curious, ironic

From July 12 to July 22: dreamy, stressed, sensitive

HEALTH

Many cancer sicknesses are psychosomatic (due to durations of melancholy). Here they need to alternate their life conduct, meals, sleep. Diseases: anemia, lack of fluid in tissues or vice versa its stasis, dry pores and skin, weakened lungs, predisposition to cough and colds, tuberculosis, pleurisy (it's miles hard for such a person to tolerate dry and warm weather), belly problems, jaundice, colitis.

Frequent mood changes in Cancer signal occur beneath the affect of the Moon, which now and again results in deep depression. Fortunately, no longer for long. Cancer is a pessimist by way of nature, deep down inside the soul remains honest, very touchy and alert. It is well worth to offend him and he'll pass into his shell, stop responding to the letters and calls.

Emotional instability, fear of intimate relationships, lack of friendliness, increased experience of hazard, tension, frequent despair, negative reminiscence. Can experience unsatisfied, with issue endures the pressure and tension associated with conversation. He is prone to melancholy, pessimism, neuroses and intellectual disorders.

CHARACTER

Its symbol is claws. The signal is ruled through the Moon, giving to Cancer emotionality, a positive thriller or even infantilism. Outwardly, he looks dim: melancholic, does now not try to be inside the highlight. For individuals who have been born under this sun signal is characterised through a choice for internal improvement, self-analysis. They have a subtle soul, a distinctly developed subconscious. He reacts strongly to any stress, aggression. He is calm when there is a tender emotional environment round.

The lifestyles of Cancer is vivid, extensive, it seems to absorb it, conquering the space round itself, creating his very own house, each time he is. He divides people into his very own and others' by way of their emotional mind-set toward himself, that is why the life for him is a field of warfare.

Cancer creates a great relationships with cherished ones. Home, family, relatives are very important to him. If the whole thing is ideal with the youngsters and the house, then the entirety else will observe, for Cancer the primary motivation is domestic and circle of relatives.

Positive developments of man or woman: susceptibility, sensitivity, romanticism, instinct, emotionality, staying power, duty, financial system, thrift, caring, affection for circle of relatives and domestic, gentleness, shyness, restraint, rich creativeness.

Negative character developments: irritability, violent reactions, a tendency to exaggerate, fears, hysteria, cowardice, touchiness, capriciousness, impermanence, laziness, grumbling, stubbornness, passivity, indecision, arrogance.

WHAT TO GIFT?

Cancers pretty respect own family, domestic comfort, so they'll surely like presents associated with home comfort, with family values, traditions, some thing in order to help to unite the circle of relatives of Cancer, cheer up all its members. The gift ought to be a wonder, because Cancers react very sensitively to the attitude of people closer to them, they trust that it's far worth them simplest once to want some thing aloud, and a actual friend will bear in mind this and gift the coveted gift to him. Ideal gifts are for domestic items, tools related to outdoor undertaking. Sentimental Cancers can be glad with any present which could decorate and create coziness in their beloved home. By the manner, they appreciate presents made with your very own palms - a patchwork duvet, a knitted sweater.

FEAR - go away their residence

Cancers are distinctly shy, impressionable and inclined, regularly locked in themselves. They are terrified of open doorways, closed area, intellectual issues, inside which there's a fear of congestion with crowd. They try to live of their protection zone, an area in which nobody and not anything can harm them. Cancers sense safe in a place most effective to which they're accustomed.

PROFFESION

In young people Cancer doesn't want to become person. The international is restricted by using most important needs: hunger, thirst, sleep. They are ready until the destiny comes to a decision for them what's going to they do. A lot of them pass via their parent's steps.

Cancers choose to work in very acquainted sphere, the work connecting with youngsters, animals, meals, garments, water, with drinks at all. From them there are good expert in breeding horses, puppies, kindergarten body of workers, musicians, instructors, writers, scientists, historians, business region, children's docs, personnel of numerous social institutions, tourism, publishing homes.

MONEY

Cancer is one of the most cash and thrifty representatives signs and symptoms of the zodiac. For this signal of zodiac money take vicinity the main region, so he tirelessly ready to earn them. It's very important for Cancer to have some savings, some economic or assets "airbag". They indiscriminately pull the whole thing to home, buy, and only then determine what to do about it. But on the equal time, Cancer are generous and noble, handing out pointless matters to negative and needy family.

Cancers do no longer threat cash and do now not waste them, they pick out the maximum dependable investments. Such forethought and thrift clearly multiplies their welfare.

LOVE

A awesome significance for Cancer has his associate, he's his foundation. He is orientated on his partner and also is very belong to him, try to keep in thoughts the connection even after loss of life or divorce. With regard to partnership, subordination and domination is very egocentric. The topic "Who is the eldest?" – is painful for him, although he tries not to show it. Cancer in emotions is owner and jealous, can without difficulty fall in love, safe their own family, secure their domestic. It's very easy to take them away, they may be led, however they may by no means go away the circle of relatives. At the identical time he is amorous and concern to emotional impact. He can not to give not an answer to the warmth, to the urge, to the affection - will always make a step to the meeting.

They are best in mattress, but they want to have emotional include any sexual act. They are awaiting an extraordinary love, understandable, placing, supporting, in return they may provide themselves completely and surround the companion with tenderness.

They are ideal in the event that they sense themselves cherished and they may be the toughest if they don't sense the affection, live in this example in infrequently and horrible lifestyles.

Their inner lifestyles depends on their success in mother and father. He loves children and guys are very attached to kids.

SEXUALITY

In an intimate existence, Cancer cannot be known as too temperamental or imaginative lover, but he is perfectly capable of sense or even to bet the desires of his companion. In mattress, he's capable of be mild and tactful, and is prepared to make every effort to provide pleasure to a loved one. Also don't forget that Cancer is an esthete and a connoisseur of consolation. In love, it's miles no much less critical to the outside entourage, starting from snug furniture and finishing with suitable tune. You can be certain that he will tastefully arrange his love nest, creating an intimate environment.

COUNTRY

Cancer is a sign of humanism, purity and the protection of traditions. It is to these characteristics that India corresponds. Cancers are individualists, they're vulnerable, cordial and type. But if someone makes a decision to encroach on their territory, they will pass at the attack. The nationalities that inhabit the "nations of Cancer", ordinarily, are wealthy spiritually. It is in these international locations that religions and mystery teachings are born. The different characteristic of the material lifestyles of those international locations is the difference from very wealthy to extraordinarily terrible, however this isn't their fundamental priority. Therefore, the high-quality nations for Cancer are: India, Holland, Denmark, Canada, New Zealand, Paraguay and Scotland.

LEO - "Authority and power"
Influence: Sun
Symbols: leo
Colors: orange, light brown, golden
Stones: ruby
Metal: gold
Talismans: the Lion
Happy days: Sunday
Unsuccessful days: Saturday
From July 23 to August 12: scrupulous and really appropriate natures, picky, loves the rite
From August 13 to August 23: strong natures, powerful, loving and worshiping authorities and command

www.ingramcontent.com/pod-product-compliance
Lightning Source LLC
Chambersburg PA
CBHW071342120626
46546CB00002B/658